Barcode in Back

‖‖ ‖ ‖‖‖‖‖‖ ‖ ‖ ‖ ‖‖‖‖‖‖‖‖‖‖‖‖ ‖‖ ‖‖‖
W9-DBD-675

ADVERTISING

TYPES, TRENDS AND CONTROVERSIES

ADVERTISING: MEDIA, MARKETING AND CONSUMER DEMANDS

Additional books in this series can be found on Nova's website
under the Series tab.

Additional E-books in this series can be found on Nova's website
under the E-books tab.

ADVERTISING

TYPES, TRENDS AND CONTROVERSIES

EVELYN P. MANN
EDITOR

Nova Science Publishers, Inc.
New York

Library of Congress Cataloging-in-Publication Data

Advertising : types, trends, and controversies / editors, Evelyn P. Mann.
    p. cm.
  Includes bibliographical references and index.
   ISBN 978-1-61324-679-5 (hardcover : alk. paper)   1.   Advertising. 2.   Advertising--New products. 3.   Consumer behavior. I. Mann, Evelyn P.
   HF5823.A453 2011
   659.1--dc22
                        2011015358

Published by Nova Science Publishers, Inc. †New York

CONTENTS

PREFACE

In today's cluttered media environment, advertisers are constantly in search of new ways to improve the strength and effectiveness of their advertisements. They are continuously competing for the limited attention resources of consumers. In this book, the authors present current research in the study of the types and trends of new advertising techniques. Topics discussed include the lipdub as a trend in corporate communications; interactive digitial television (IDTV) advertising; differential effects of visual and verbal elements in advertisements for new brands and extensions; the internet as an important advertising medium and children and advertising.

Chapter 1 – The electronic provision of services and the use of consumer loyalty schemes means that organisations can now track transactions and profile consumers. Organisations can now monitor valued customers and offer inducements, or monitor vulnerable consumers and issue consumer warnings. In addition to a consumer's profile, technology may also reveal a consumer's location.

Hence there is an emerging capability for organisations to specifically target individual consumers at specific locations with their advertising (e.g. when nearing point of sale). The cost of this advertising may be comparatively cheap (e.g. internet SPAM), with the consumer potentially bearing a greater proportion of the cost (e.g. premium SMS). This chapter considers factors that may influence consumer response to recommender agents.

It seems that degree of risk, time pressure, as well as the consumers' impulse control, intellectual attainment, and mental status will influence compliance with recommender agents. Using loyalty schemes and tracking transactions may also give some indication of consumers who exceed their affordable limits. This raises the question as to how best this technology can be applied to the concept of consumer protection – corporate ethical practices balancing marketing against consumer protection.

Chapter 2 – Lately the authors are seeing how different kinds of institutions are uploading on the Internet a sort of video clip recorded by a group of people who lip sync to a song, act and dance while the camera follows them through the facilities of the institution they belong to: these are the more and more popular *lipdub* videos. This new communication practice has introduced an important change in the way of approaching institutional communication. The *lipdub* embraces a high component of creativity that allows institutions to showcase a different perspective of themselves which influences the corporate image to a large extent. However, this influence may become also a double edged sword if the performance is not professionally done considering the institution culture and philosophy. That is, although at first sight the *lipdub* seems to be an effective, informal, creative and even funny way of promoting an institution it can cause a serious damage difficult to make up. Private and public companies, Universities, Student Residences and other institutions are taking advantage from this trendy communication tool with the aim of enhancing their image and meantime attracting new clients, students or potential employees. In this work the authors look into the *lipdub* concept, explain its effects on corporate image, assess its value for institutions from a communication perspective by analysing consequences for them and, finally, the authors suggest a practical guide to perform a successful *lipdub* when advisable. Illustrative examples will be used along the content analysis.

Chapter 3 – In today's cluttered media environment, advertisers are constantly in search for new ways to improve the strength and effectiveness of their advertisements. They are continuously competing for the limited attention resources of consumers, declaring a so called "war for eye balls" (Schiessl et al., 2003). Contrary to the traditional, sequential formats of advertising, new technologies like Interactive Digital Television (IDTV) allow simultaneous exposure to media content and interactive advertising content using on-screen placements, television banners (Cauberghe and De Pelsmacker, 2008) or split-screen advertising (Chowdhury et al., 2007). Therefore, it is important to understand which factors determine viewer attention in today's cluttered and increasingly complex media environment.

In this study, viewers are simultaneously exposed to both an interactive advertisement and a program context using IDTV technology. By doing so, they are forced to divide their attention between both information sources.

This may lead to cognitive interference and consequently to less attention devoted to the advertisement. Using eye tracking, the authors study the role of program environment, more specifically how a thematically (in)congruent program affects both visual attention to an interactive ad and involvement with the ad message. Also, the authors investigate how congruence moderates the effect of cognitive load resulting from time pressure, while interacting with the interactive ad.

Results show that when viewers are simultaneously exposed to a congruent context (i.e. the program and the interactive advertisement are thematically congruent), they devote more visual attention to the ad and jump more between the ad and the program than when the ad is processed in an incongruent context. Viewers are hindered and distracted by the fact that the information in the ad merges with the program context, therefore needing more time to disentangle both. Processing the information in an incongruent context, on the other hand, is less interfering and thus requires less time. Also, time pressure significantly reduces ad viewing time in the congruent context, while it does not affect viewing time in the incongruent situation. Further, results show a higher involvement with the ad message in the incongruent that in the congruent condition but increasing time pressure, on the other hand, does not appear to affect message involvement.

Chapter 4 – The present study applies schema theory, the incongruity principle and the persuasion knowledge model to study consumer responses to visual and verbal elements in new products advertisements. Advertisements containing no, product related or (general) non-product related visuals, and no, basic or extended verbal information were tested for a line extension and a new brand.

The results show that brand strategy significantly moderates the effectiveness of verbal and visual elements in advertising. For new brands, non-product related visuals lead to the most negative responses.

For line extensions, the absence of visuals significantly reduces the attitude toward the ad. Consistent with enrichment, the added value of information is stronger for line extensions than for new brands. Implications and suggestions for further research are discussed.

Chapter 5 – Many consumers do not buy what they dream about. Thus, to attract the consumer without creating disappointment, the authors need to reconcile dream and reality.

However, the compromise between dream and reality is difficult to achieve because it can differ significantly according to individuals, culture and countries. The definition of an efficient global strategy therefore leads us to examine these differences. In this study, advertising discourse is used as a means to reconcile the gap between the bought and the dream product. Means-end chains make it possible to determine the buying and the dream processes.

A clustering analysis method, MPC method (Aurifeille, 2004), was used to determine reconcilable processes. Results suggest that narcissistic people are an ideal target for global marketing strategies since they do not feel a gap: one single advertising discourse corresponds to both the bought and the dream product.

Among individuals who have a significant gap, only less narcissistic and older people can bear a wide gap. The structure of the discourse which reconciles both the bought and the dream product is examined.

Chapter 6 – In all circumstances television advertisements affect children of different age and gender groups in terms of consumption. Because of the ease to affect and lead children, advertisers consider them as the target audience. Today, since television advertisements have an important and effective role in the conscious raising of children who will be socialized as the consumers of the future, we are confronted by the imperative to focus on television ads. For this reason, this study has been planned and conducted with the aim of determining the effects of television advertisements on primary school age children and understanding their attitude towards advertisements. The sample of this research is constituted by 225 students, who are selected by random sampling method from the 6th, 7th and 8th grades of 5 primary schools within Ankara city territories. The results of the research show that girls watch more television advertisements than boys do (p<.05) and that the ratio of those who "always" watch television advertisements, decline with the increase in education level. Furthermore, at the end of the research it was found that children, be it a girl or a boy at any education level, want to possess the goods and services that they see on television advertisements. However, it was also seen that there is a high ratio of those who think that goods and services that they purchase sometimes carry the characteristics stated in the advertisements. Moreover, the findings of the research also indicate that while most of the children agree with the fact that advertisements are "entertaining" and "effective in shopping," a considerable number of children think that advertisements cause prodigality. More critical than that, findings pinpoint that the ratio of those who think that advertisements are "honest and real" decline while the ratio (p<.05) of those who think that advertisements are "misguiding and deceptive" increase with the increase in grade level.

Chapter 7 – The internet is an important medium for advertising; web advertisements provide income for web sites, online e-mail services and search engines, and are considerably less expensive than other forms of advertising. Advertisements are intended to influence the behavior of the internet user, but in some cases may expose the viewer to images or issues that are not age appropriate.

Advertisements are common on social network sites, yet information from companies may not always be openly identified as an advertisement. For example, when a user indicates "liking" some online content or becoming a member of a particular group, they may be later targeted for specific messages from advertisers or employees of the company selling the product.

Young users of social network web pages, such as Facebook, may not realize that if they indicate they "like" an alcohol product (or become a member of a related group) they are more likely to receive messages from alcohol companies. In this commentary, the authors discuss the reach of internet advertising, the marketing of alcohol products on the internet, and its possible influence on youth.

In: Advertising
Editor: Evelyn P. Mann

ISBN 978-1-61324-679-5
© 2012 Nova Science Publishers, Inc.

Chapter 1

HUMAN FACTORS DETERMINING
CONSUMER RESPONSE TO RECOMMENDERS

J. G. Phillips[1], R. P. Ogeil[1] and A. Blaszczynski[2]
[1]School of Psychology and Psychiatry, Monash University,
VIC 3800, Australia
[2]School of Psychology, University of Sydney, NSW 2006, Australia

ABSTRACT

The electronic provision of services and the use of consumer loyalty schemes means that organisations can now track transactions and profile consumers. Organisations can now monitor valued customers and offer inducements, or monitor vulnerable consumers and issue consumer warnings. In addition to a consumer's profile, technology may also reveal a consumer's location.

Hence there is an emerging capability for organisations to specifically target individual consumers at specific locations with their advertising (e.g. when nearing point of sale). The cost of this advertising may be comparatively cheap (e.g. internet SPAM), with the consumer potentially bearing a greater proportion of the cost (e.g. premium SMS). This chapter considers factors that may influence consumer response to recommender agents.

It seems that degree of risk, time pressure, as well as the consumers' impulse control, intellectual attainment, and mental status will influence compliance with recommender agents. Using loyalty schemes and tracking transactions may also give some indication of consumers who exceed their affordable limits. This raises the question as to how best this technology can be applied to the concept of consumer protection – corporate ethical practices balancing marketing against consumer protection.

HUMAN FACTORS DETERMINING CONSUMER RESPONSE TO RECOMMENDERS

Organisations seek to deliver services over the internet to extend their "reach" and reduce operating costs and overheads. Unfortunately the same facilities also extend to an organisation's competitors. As an organisation's competitors are only another mouse click away (Nielsen, 2000) organisations have sought to develop a competitive edge by ensuring that their website is more usable (Nielsen, 2000) or attractive (Tractinsky, Katz, and Ikar, 2000). With the proliferation of websites and offerings, recommender technologies (Resnick and Varian, 1997) seek to function as personalised shop assistants (Schafer, Konstan, and Riedl, 2001) assisting consumers to make their purchases. The bulk of research addresses the design of such recommenders. The present paper addresses factors associated with consumer response to such decisional support.

The growth of the world wide web has meant consumers can be overwhelmed by the wealth of information, applications and products (Park and Lee, 2008). To assist consumers navigate an organisation's website, decision aids in the form of recommender technologies have been developed to assist consumers (Resnick and Varian, 1997). The recommendations can take the form of *related products* or lists of *top 10 sellers* (Schafer, Konstan, and Riedl, 2001). Other recommendations are of the form: *"people who bought this product also bought"*. The development of recommender technology is intended to assist consumers to navigate an inventory, convert browsers into buyers, increase customer loyalty, and increase cross-selling (Schafer, Konstan, and Riedl, 2001).

These interactions with consumers can take the form of a Push (e.g. emailed recommendations when a customer is not at the website) or a Pull (e.g. requests to evaluate a product) (Schafer, Konstan, and Riedl, 2001). The price of such advertising may be relatively cheap in the case of emails (Kraut, Sunder, Telang, and Morris, 2005), but can be more expensive in the case of premium SMS, where the consumer is effectively paying for advertising

(Mahatanankoon, Wen, and Lim, 2005). Hence these unsolicited forms of messaging attract the interests of legislators seeking to restrict Spam.

A diverse range of recommenders have been developed that operate on different forms of input (Montaner, Lopez, and De La Rosa, 2003). The two main classes of recommenders are: 1) Content Based; and 2) Collaborative Filters. *Content Based recommenders* operate upon product descriptors such as keywords. Such recommenders operate better on material that has a textual element (Montaner, Lopez, and De La Rosa, 2003). The more information that a customer supplies about the products they are seeking, the more useful the assistance rendered. These recommenders are suitable in assisting new customers.

Collaborative Filters seek similarities between a consumer and other consumers (user to user) or between a product and other products (item to item) (Schafer, Konstan, and Riedl, 2001). These recommenders can perform better upon material that is less amenable to text based processing such as music and film (Montaner, Lopez, and De La Rosa, 2003; Perugini, Gonçalves, and Fox, 2004). As the approaches are to some extent complementary, hybrid systems have been developed where each approach can address some of the problems of the other approach (Montaner, Lopez, and De La Rosa, 2003). For instance, Content Based recommenders are less able to deal with subjective information, and as they focus upon past history, are less likely to offer a consumer something new (McSherry, 2002). In contrast a Collaborative Filter needs to learn a consumers' interests, and initially performs poorly with a new user, and may have difficulty with sparsity of data sets, particularly if a consumer has an unusual profile. Again the more information that a consumer supplies, the better the assistance rendered.

Information derived from the consumer can be in the form of active enquiry, or can arise from prior customer history (Montaner, Lopez, and De La Rosa, 2003). This information can take the form of explicit ratings, or can evolve implicitly from tracking of consumer activity such as whether the consumer was searching, or browsing, the time spent viewing a page, and whether this was the first or second time a page was clicked on (Kim, Yum, Song, and Kim, 2005).

Recommendations arising from Content Based recommenders can take the form of related products or genres. Recommendations from Collaborative Filters are made by drawing similarities between the present consumer and past consumers, and take the form of "people who bought this product also bought that product" (Schafer, Konstan, and Riedl, 2001).

RECOMMENDATIONS OVER TIME

Recommender systems operate upon previous history of consumer behaviour, and while such predictors may apply for the majority of purposes there can be some circumstances that are difficult to predict (Taleb, 2007). Indeed, as recommenders interact with a consumer over a period of time, it is likely that the consumer's interest will vary to some degree (Montaner, Lopez, and De La Rosa, 2003). In addition, some consumer behaviour can be seasonal or event driven (Schafer, Konstan, and Riedl, 2001), hence some researchers have sought to develop recommenders that respond to consumer trends (Min and Han, 2005), or otherwise adapt to changing interests by applying a time window or a "forgetting function" (Montaner, Lopez, and De La Rosa, 2003).

Kim, Yum, Song, and Kim (2005) tracked consumer behaviour on a experimental e-commerce site. They tracked the type of click (searching, browsing), the number of visits, the length of reading time, whether the site was bookmarked, the number of clicks on a product, whether the item was placed in a basket, and whether an item was purchased. They considered the probability of purchase as a function of consumer behaviour. Kim, Yum, Song, and Kim (2005) observed that a direct search followed by a click led to a 0.316 likelihood of purchase. In addition, as the number of times a consumer clicked on an item increased, the likelihood of purchase increased. Likelihood of purchase from the first click was 0.076, but following a second click, the likelihood of purchase of 0.295, while the probability increased to 0.316 with more than 2 clicks.

Perugini, Gonçalves, and Fox (2004) argued that social comparison and referral are natural consumer behaviours. Hence they discussed the degree of connectivity in social networks. An early empirical demonstration of these social connections was performed by Milgram (1967). Milgram (1967) used a chain letter methodology, in which he asked people to forward a letter to others with whom they were on a first name basis. The task of each person in the chain was to forward the letter to someone they knew that could eventually deliver the letter to a target person. Milgram found that a randomly selected starting individual was connected to a target person by no more than six intermediate acquaintances (the so-called six degrees of separation). Perugini, Gonçalves, and Fox (2004) discussed a number of techniques to model social networks. In particular, they considered the distance (number of successive nodes) between consumers in social networks as a possible metric of potential consumer recommendation influence.

Leskovec, Adamic, and Huberman (2007) actually monitored the process of recommendation. They offered consumers a 10% discount if someone else purchased on the basis of an emailed recommendation that the consumer made. They recorded the 16 million recommendations made by 4 million individuals for half a million products. The number and pattern of these recommendations was then analysed. This discount promotion led to an almost linear growth in the number of customers over time, and allowed the profiling of networks of consumers. However the number of recommendations made did not directly convert into purchases, and this varied with the nature of the product under consideration. For books, two received recommendations was associated with the greatest likelihood of a purchase, with subsequent additional recommendations having less effect. For DVDs, ten received recommendations was associated with the greatest likelihood of a purchase, with additional recommendations having less impact. If the recommendations were sent by the same person, the initial recommendation had the most influence. Subsequent recommendations from the same source tended to have less influence upon a consumer. Indeed a recommendation had its' greatest influence on the day of receipt, with a lesser probability of purchase on subsequent days. In addition, recommendations and purchases followed a circadian pattern, with fewer recommendations and purchases occuring around 10am. Such observations indicate that a recommendation and subsequent purchase can be a dynamic and time-dependent process.

RECOMMENDATIONS IN SPACE

Recommenders were initially developed in environments where static users connected with the internet through computer workstations. However with wireless connectivity it is more likely that a consumer is in motion. Indeed, more people have mobile phones than access to the internet via personal computers (Boyera, 2006). The increase in portable personal devices has caused companies to investigate the effectiveness of selling and buying through mobile devices, a domain of business referred to as m-Commerce (McManus and Scornavacca, 2005). Wireless platforms are especially of interest in mobile marketing because recommendations can be made instantaneously, become more personal as a mobile is not a shared device like a home computer and recommendations are not restricted to a wired network (McManus and Scornavacca, 2005). It should be noted that mobile recommenders differ from Spam text messages. Mobile recommenders require the user to create an account online and the user controls how and when they wish to receive recommendations. Otherwise such systems tend to function in contravention of the various Spam prevention acts.

Mobile interfaces can be cumbersome, lacking the input devices and computing power to navigate complex graphics in most webpages (Piyasena and Chan, 2008). Hence applications (Apps) and recommenders have been developed to support mobile phones (Preece, 2010). Given the capacity to locate mobile phones from Global Positioning Systems or from the network, such systems can tailor their recommendations to incorporate geographical information (e.g. Hinze and Quan, 2009). Internet based recommendation systems have not traditionally incorporated consumer location (Yang, Cheng, and Dia, 2008), even though there is a technical capability (see http://www. ip2location.com/). However recommender systems can now take into account the location of a consumer's mobile phone.

Mobile recommender systems differ in the way they make recommendations and how a user's location is monitored. Recommendations can be sent directly to the person's mobile device via SMS, MMS or Bluetooth, or the user can use their mobile device and explicitly request a recommendation of a product. The location of the user can be determined by centralised or decentralised methods.

Centralised methods use signals from the device beamed out to deployed receivers to determine the user's location. Decentralised methods, such as Global Positioning Service (GPS), are usually "opt in" and involve the user receiving signals on their mobile device from beacons indicating the user's location (Yang, Cheng, and Dia, 2008). For instance, Yang, Cheng, and Dia (2008) developed a system that can take into account consumers' interests or needs, and supply consumers with information as to vendors that are in their geographical neighbourhood. They reported greater consumer satisfaction for recommendations that took into account both content and distance.

Recommender systems typically employ decentralised methods so that the user controls whether the application has access to their location. Applications using decentralised methods have been tested which send messages such as the location of nearby sale items (Yuan and Tsao, 2003), and link to nearby vendor's web-pages (Yang et al., 2008). Centralised methods have also been used to send messages as users walk past vendors that have a receiver in shop front (Aalto et al., 2004). Hence the consumer is increasingly a moving target that can be monitored and appealed to.

DYNAMIC ENVIRONMENTS

Our own research has considered the use of decisional support in dynamic and uncertain environments. In our laboratory paradigm participants are required to play a computerised game of Blackjack. Decisional support is variously supplied in terms of advice that serves to minimise player losses (e.g. the Basic system), or advice that confers an advantage to players (i.e. card counting) (Thorp, 1966). In such tasks it is possible to vary issues such as time pressure and risk, and monitor compliance with the decision aid, and measure the influence of the manipulations upon consumer confidence in terms of wagering behaviour.

Such studies indicate that the provision of decisional support increases willingness to wager. These observations support contentions that recommenders encourage consumer behaviour (Shafer, Konstan, and Riedl, 2001). For instance, in a game of computerised blackjack, Chau, Phillips and Von Baggo (2000) considered the effect of online decisional support upon players' wagering. They observed a tendency for players to wager more in the presence of decisional support. Subsequent studies found that wagering can significantly increase with decisional support. For instance an unpublished study by O'Hare, Phillips, and Moss (2005) observed higher levels of wagering in the presence of decisional support (Basic). This was also demonstrated by Phillips and Ogeil (2007). Philips and Ogeil (2007) found players were more likely to bet more in the presence of decisional support (Basic) in a higher stakes condition than the low stakes condition. Indeed, there was also some evidence that participants relied upon advice after a dose of alcohol bringing them to a blood alcohol concentration of 0.05%. Players seemed to spend more time attending to advice after consuming alcohol. It seems that participants were more likely to use advice when they were impaired or when there was more at stake.

The time dependent nature of influence has been noted in the previous sections (Leskovec, Adamic, and Huberman, 2007). It seems decisional support can be supplied, but it may not be attended to. For instance, Chau and Phillips (1995) supplied advice that was supposed to minimise loss (Basic), but was actually non-functional. Although there were indications that participants initially attended to the advice, after some exposure they ceased attending to the advice. An additional unpublished study by Lok (2008) used advice that actually minimised loss. This study suggested that the processing of the decisional support requires time and imposes an additional processing load on players. During a computerised Blackjack task, Lok (2008) exposed participants to decisional support for one, three, or seven seconds. The influence of the aid increased with greater exposure time, but only up to a point. Most of the effect of the decision aid had occurred by three seconds. Apparently participants need time to appreciate and utilise a decision aid, but continued exposure may not guarantee further influence.

O'Hare, Phillips and Moss (2009) used the Blackjack paradigm to address consumer response to advice. O'Hare, Phillips and Moss (2009) monitored education levels and logical reasoning ability. In this study Basic advice was supplied that simply served to minimise loss. Compliance with this advice was associated with logical reasoning ability. Less well educated individuals were more confident when decisional support was available. Better educated individuals used the decision aid to avoid errors. Interactions between use of advice and level of ability have been observed elsewhere (Hu and Pu, 2010).

It appears the effect of a decision aid upon player behaviour is not simple. Phillips and Amrhein (1989) examined wagering when players controlled their own cards, in comparison to decisional support that played for them (a simple "never bust" algorithm). Players bet more when they could control their own cards and use their own strategies. In addition players wagered significantly less on an algorithm when they were losing. Such data suggest that players prefer their own personalised strategies, and are more prepared to abandon advice in the face of losses. When providing online advice to participants, Chau, Phillips and Von Baggo (2000) found participants that were provided with online advice initially felt the outcome of their gambling was less likely to be due to luck, and were less optimistic as to the outcomes of the next set of hands to be played. Indeed others have observed that reliance upon decision aids appears to vary as a function of the perceived reliability of the aid (Parasuraman and Riley, 1997) or the transparency of its' operation (McSherry, 2005).

ONLINE TRUST

With the pervasiveness and ubiquitousness of the internet and mobile computing, people now have access to services, shops and their social networks at all hours of the day. The internet has allowed people to communicate cheaply (Resnick and Zeckhauser, 2002) and interact with strangers to complete transactions whom they are unlikely to ever meet (Resnick and Zeckhauser, 2002). However, with this increased exposure that is provided by the internet also comes important considerations including privacy, security and trust issues. Indeed there are many varied views on what constitutes 'online' trust and what factors are important in identifying it.

In considering purchases made via the internet, Wang and Emurian (2005) identified three integral components of online trust. Firstly, both the consumer and the merchant must trust each other, and also the technology used. Not only must the internet itself be trusted by both parties for a transaction to take place, but the platforms and security where customers provide personal details must also be reliable and secure (Ang et al., 2001). Secondly, when making a purchase online, a consumer must believe that their details will not be misused or stolen. Integrity within an online environment involves transparency in that the merchant will keep to their promises (Gefen, 2002), and also that a merchant will take reasonable steps to rectify a problem if a product does not satisfy a consumer (Ang et al., 2001). Thirdly, online trust involves a building of relationships, such that after a purchase has been made, consumers will return to browse for other items for sale (Wang and Emurian, 2005).

There are similarities between online and offline trust. To be successful, an online organisation or website must be deemed as having a good reputation, with the appearance of their website being one key component (Beldad et al., 2010). Graphical design features and usability are vital to online merchants because they provide both a consumer's first look, and hence assessment of reputation, as well as the interface where purchases are made. The content design, including availability of informational components either text or pictorial and social cue design e.g. representative photographs or video clips on the site help to build reputation, and hence trust with consumers (Wang and Emurian, 2005). If consumers are unable to navigate pages, or the system is hard to use they are unlikely to enter credit card details and make a purchase.

Jarvenpaa, Tractinsky, and Vitale (2000) examined factors important to buyers (n=184) making a travel or a book purchase on-line. They found that the size of the online business had a positive relationship with trustworthiness measures. Specifically, those websites who displayed larger sales volumes on their website were more likely to be trusted by buyers. In addition, Jaevenpaa et al (2000) noted that larger organisations may also be preferred as they are deemed as having the necessary expertise in terms of security, software systems, and would be more likely to compensate unhappy buyers. Hence, for trust to exist, consumers must believe that the seller has both the ability and the motivation to deliver the goods.

In addition to design features, comments or reviews by other buyers may also influence perceptions of online trust. For example, Ba and Pavlou (2002) found that positive and negative feedback about a seller were important in deciding whether experienced e-bay buyers ($n=95$) would do business with that seller. Specifically, positive feedback was associated with greater levels of trust. In addition to asking buyers about their online shopping habits, other research has considered the feedback provided on e-bay itself. Resnick and Zeckhauser (2002) reported that feedback is provided more than 50% of the time following a purchase, and that a seller's subsequent 'reputation' which is built on this feedback was an indication of their future performance in terms of sales. In addition, there was a high correlation between a buyer and a seller's feedback following a sale. For buyers, only 0.6% of all feedback was negative, 0.3% was neutral, while 99.1% was positive. When sellers were positive about a buyer, 99.7% of buyers were positive in return. This high level of positive feedback suggests that such information allows consumers to distinguish between trustworthy and untrustworthy sellers and also encourages transparency of sellers or online businesses, and serves to discourage those who may wish to be untrustworthy (Resnick and Zeckhauser, 2002).

Chen (2008) found that people were favourably disposed to, and were more likely to trust *consumer recommendations* than advice supplied by the website owner. The concern is that the website owner might be providing recommendations that are biassed. Indeed there are indications that there are attempts to influence recommendations. Lam, Frankowski and Riedl (2006) reported an instance where Amazon accidentally revealed the identities of people making recommendations about books (http://www.nytimes.com/2004/ 02/14/ technology/14AMAZ.html). A *high proportion of recommendations were actually by authors praising their own work*, or criticising the works of other authors. People that attempt to influence sales without disclosing their relationship with the vendor are called "Shills". Hence attempts to bias and influence the performance of recommenders are sometimes called "Shilling attacks" (Lam, Frankowski, and Riedl, 2006). Even though there are attempts to recognise and thwart this behaviour (e.g. Mehta and Nejdl, 2009), such attempts can be compromised by issues of anonymity and privacy (Lam, Frankowski, and Riedl, 2006).

PRIVACY

Issues of online privacy may be divided into 4 areas of concern (Lenhart, 2000):

a) improper acquisition of personal details (e.g. preference tracking);
b) improper use of information (i.e. 3rd party distribution);
c) privacy invasion (e.g. direct mailing);
d) improper storage (i.e. no opting out).

In a recent review, Beldad et al. (2010) argue that the two biggest risks with making an online purchase are financial in that the money staked may be lost, and the threat of a privacy breach, such that personal details including credit card numbers, name, address or telephone numbers are stolen. In addition, there are privacy concerns relating to junk e-mail marketing organisations, web-based advertisements that may track user preferences or history and malicious programs that may be able to obtain personal information or credit details (Wang et al., 1998).

National surveys have previously revealed that such concerns are warranted. The PIP Project in the USA found that 68% of people express concern about revealing their credit card or other personal details over the web and that while 48% had made an internet purchase, 3% reported being cheated or had their credit details stolen (Wang and Emurian, 2005). The risk of a privacy breach is that 3rd parties could intercept and misuse or modify any information that is sent, and the information could be passed onto other organisations without the consent of the individual (Horst et al., 2007).

Familiarity with both the internet and with making online purchases are also likely to influence online trust (Boyd, 2003). For example George (2002) found that a person's likelihood to make purchases online was influenced by their attitude towards online shopping. Indeed, Lenhart (2000) reported that more internet experience was associated with more positive views on the trustworthiness of the internet (r=.298), that increased trustworthiness was associated with more positive attitude to making internet purchases (r=.347), and that intent to purchase was associated with purchasing (r=.394). In addition, there was also a relationship between experience and purchasing (r=.286). This suggests that as consumers gain more experience online, they will make their first purchase, and then eventually purchase more often, hence retailers may attract more people by addressing privacy issues. Despite this, these correlations are not high, suggesting that privacy itself is not likely to drive whether people will purchase online and other factors including accessibility and convenience may be taken into account.

USEFULNESS VERSUS RISK

Despite the prevalence of e-commerce applications, customers are reluctant to provide sensitive information online. While people are generally comfortable providing preferences and other general information via the web, they are uncomfortable providing personal or credit card details (Suh and Han, 2002). These reservations are due in part to customer's distrust of internet based security or the notion of risk.

In the internet environment, remote users from all over the world are potentially able to access critical files on other people's computers (Suh and Han, 2002). Internet banking is an example of a potentially risky venture. As the parties involved in the transaction are not in the same place, customers cannot directly observe the transaction as if it were carried out by a bank teller, and they cannot depend on the cues usually provided within this context: e.g. physical proximity, body signals of teller, immediate receipts upon transactions, access to help (Suh and Han, 2002). Suh and Han (2002) studied 845 people online with respect to online trust issues. They found that usefulness, usability and attitude towards internet banking had a significant impact on trust.

RECOMMENDERS AND PRIVACY

Recommenders seek to deliver personalised assistance (Schafer, Konstan, and Riedl, 2001). Hence recommenders do not function as well if the consumer is not known to the system (the cold start problem) or if the consumer does not volunteer information about themselves (sparsity) (Montaner, Lopez, and De La Rosa, 2003). If there is not much information in the system about a consumer, it is difficult to determine their interests. To address this problem recommenders seek to draw similarities between the active consumer and other consumers (Perugini, Gonçalves, and Fox, 2004). Some systems seek to overcome such problems by implicitly inferring consumer lifestyle from demographic information (Giaglis and Lekakos, 2006), or by explicitly requesting responses on rating scales that can then draw inferences as to an individual's personality (Hu and Pu, 2010). More information can lead to better recommendations, however the information retained within the system can potentially identify a consumer and locate a consumer (Christen, 2009). For instance, it is estimated that gender, age, and zip code can uniquely identify individuals (Lam, Frankowski, and Riedl, 2006), and there are concerns that such information can be leveraged out of recommenders to identify individuals (Ramakrishnan, Keller, Mirza, Grama, and Karypis, 2001) with subsequent risk of identity theft. In addition IP addresses can potentially locate a consumer (e.g. http://iplocationfinder.com/) such that they can be targetted in a variety of ways (Christen, 2009). Thus there can be a tradeoff between privacy and quality of service (Lam, Frankowski, and Riedl, 2006).

Indeed there may not be a one-to-one relationship between recommender and consumer. Systems that deliver personalised advertising may be viewed by third persons (Ali and van Stam, 2004). This may occur when the recommender is delivering personalised information in public places (Finn, 2005), such as would occur for computer workstations in class rooms, mobile phones on public transport, or televisions (Ali and van Stam, 2004). Where this personalised advertising reveals a person's hobbies, sexual orientation, or interest in gambling there is a potential loss of privacy (see Saling and Phillips, 2010). Social networking sites are a current source of problems.

SOCIAL NETWORKING

In the US, 24% of adults have visited social networking sites in the past 30 days (Ipsos Insight, 2007) and one of the most popular, Facebook has over 70 million active users, half of whom log in daily (Lewis et al., 2008). Social network sites penetrate their users' everyday lives and as pervasive technology, become invisible once they are widely adopted, ubiquitous and taken for granted (Debatin et al., 2009). The most active users of social networking sites are students who use Facebook and Myspace to communicate, connect and remain in touch with others (Acquisti and Gross, 2006).

Fogel and Nehmad (2009) investigated risk taking, privacy and trust with regard to social networking sites in 205 college students. 77.6% of participants had a social network profile, with Facebook being the most popular. The majority of participants allowed anyone to view their profile (73.6%), while 86.2% had a photo of themselves displayed, 64.8% had their e-mail address visible to anyone and only 9.4% had phone number or address. 81.8% had their real name displayed. Similar research has also found that only 13% of profiles on Facebook of students at Michigan State University were restricted to 'friends' only (Ellison, Steinfield, and Lampe, 2007). Fogel and Nehmad

(2009) found that those who did have a social network site (n=159) had *higher scores on a risk taking scale* than those who did not have a profile on a social networking site, but that concerns about privacy did not differ between groups. Also those who had the profiles were more likely to share identity information with others in the future. With respect to trust, those who had a social networking page had more trust in Facebook (but interestingly not Myspace), however reasons for this were not explored in this study.

Debatin et al., (2009) argued that social networking sites have now become pervasive and this has led to unintended consequences such as privacy breaches. Specific privacy concerns regarding social networking sites include: disclosure of personal information, damaged reputation due to gossip, unwanted contact from others, stalking, background surveillance by third party data miners, hacking and identity theft. Facebook was criticised for its use of Beacon software to track user behaviour as well as the access they afforded to agencies of the state (Debatin et al., 2009). For example, the Patriot Act allows state agencies to bypass privacy settings on Facebook to look up private information of potential employees, without consent of the user.

Ellison et al. (2007) examined Facebook users' (*n*=119 college undergraduates) awareness of privacy issues (whether they knew about changing default settings, if they protected their profile and how so e.g. limiting to friends only) and unintended consequences of use. This study also examined what constituted a 'friend' on Facebook, that is, whether they knew the person personally, through mutual friends, or whether they accepted anybody who requested to be their friend. Risk was assessed via: unwanted advances, damaging gossip, personal data stolen or abused by a 3rd party and how they responded to that (e.g. restricted or deleted profile or did nothing). In addition 8 participants from the online survey were selected for in-depth interviews. Half the respondents were found to have had an account for 2 years. Of these users, 37% checked it daily, 25% checked it 3 times per day, 23% checked it 5 times per day. Also 29% reported that their Facebook account was always open or active. 18% of the sample had some negative experiences (unwanted advances, stalking, gossip, hacked), 47% had restricted access because they were cautious, 38% because they had heard concerning stories. Most people 83% reported Facebook helps with interacting with friends. Interestingly, only 69% had changed the default privacy settings on their profile (from: everyone can see), and half had restricted profile to only friends. Over 90% signed up with their real name and included gender, date of birth and hometown. This data suggests that users do not perceive social networking sites to be as risky as other transactions over the internet, such as banking, despite their potential to be. Social networking sites contain personal information such as names, address and birthdates which may be used by 3rd parties to gain access to other sensitive information.

CONSUMER PROTECTION

In order to maintain a transparent and sustainable industry it is necessary to protect consumers (Blazczynski, Ladouceur, and Shaffer, 2004; Blaszczynski, Ladouceur, Nower, and Shaffer, 2008). Previously, Blazczynski and colleagues (2004) had proposed the Reno model, which argues for a science-based approach as the foundation for socially responsible policies designed to protect consumers, minimise social harm, and maintain a sustainable industry. At the core of this model is the proposal that individuals are ultimately responsible for their behaviour, but that individuals must be made aware of all alternative choices available to them so that they can be informed consumers (Blaszczynski et al., 2008). Concurrent to this is an obligation for the providers of services to assume responsibility for acting in a responsible manner that promotes and fosters responsible consumer behaviour within the scope of government regulations and community expectations. Providers of services ought not to exploit or unfairly induce consumption of products through the use of technology. Despite this ideal, the internet is an area where there are demonstrable shortfalls, with scams (http://www. scamwatch.com/) and Spam (http://www.ftc.gov/spam/) causing problems for regulated and legitimate users (Dow, Serenko, Turel, and Wong, 2006; Whittaker, Bellotti, and Moody, 2005), and operators providing services (e.g. pornography, gambling) to areas where the services are illegal (Phillips, Ostojic, and Blaszczynski, in press), causing problems for legitimate providers of services and problems for regulatory bodies (Eadington, 2004).

The technology to assist and influence consumers has tended to outstrip the technology to protect them. Indeed such technology tends to create loopholes that challenge a jurisdiction's capability to restrict access to content (Phillips, Ostojic, and Blaszczynski, in press). Advertising of inappropriate content (e.g. tobacco) has shifted to the internet (Hrywna, Delnevo, and Lewis, 2007), and it is likely that inappropriate inducements are also being made (Sévigny, Cloutier, Pelletier, and Ladouceur, 2005). Sévigny, Cloutier, Pelletier, and Ladouceur (2005) examined the demonstration modes of 117 online gambling sites. They observed that 39% gave an unrealistic and inflated impression of the likelihood of winning in the demonstration mode. Indeed, attempts to block such activities have variously been thwarted. For instance, attempts to prohibit online gambling (USA vs Antigua and Barbuda) have been ruled as restrictions of trade (http://www.wto.org/english/tratop_e/ dispu_e/cases_e/ds285_e.htm. Whereas attempts to control pornography with the Child Online Protection Act had been declared unconstitutional, as amongst other issues it restricted freedom of speech. In such an environment there are *concerns that consumer protection information can be difficult to find on websites* (Monaghan, 2009).

A concern in recommender literature is whether advice can be trusted and whether it is biassed (Lam, Frankowski, and Riedl, 2006). It is likely that the direction of advice can influence behaviour. An unpublished study by Laughlin (2008) manipulated the direction of advice supplied, effectively biassing the advice conferred. When playing Blackjack, a strategy called Basic advises people to stand or sit depending upon the totals of the player and the dealer (Thorp, 1967). In some conditions Laughlin only applied the advice to "stand" when appropriate. In other conditions Laughlin only applied the advice to "hit" when appropriate. Directional advice tended to promote riskier wagering and decisions when people were only advised to hit, and tended to promote less risky wagering and decisions when people were only advised to stand. It is likely that such effects will vary with the perceived riskiness of the behaviour. At low risk participants tended to engage in riskier behaviour when advised to stand, and be more cautious when advised to hit. Such studies demonstrate the *potential to induce consumer purchasing behaviour, or warn vulnerable consumers.*

Howard Shaffer's group at Harvard managed to gain access to the transaction records of bwin, an online gaming provider (Shaffer, Peller, LaPlante, Nelson, and LaBrie, 2010). Shaffer's group tracked activity of online poker players (LaPlante, Kleschinsky, LaBrie, Nelson, and Shaffer, 2009), and sports gamblers (LaBrie, LaPlante, Nelson, Schumann, and Shaffer, 2007; LaPlante, Schumann, LaBrie, and Shaffer, 2008), and people gambling at an online casino (LaBrie, Kaplan, LaPlante, Nelson, and Shaffer, 2008). This was a major achievement in that it allowed researchers to address actual rather than reported gambling (Shaffer, Peller, LaPlante, Nelson, and LaBrie, 2010). In general these studies observed that the majority of individuals appeared to gamble in moderation, but the population had an appreciable skew, with a minority gambling appreciably more (Shaffer, Peller, LaPlante, Nelson, and LaBrie, 2010).

The transaction records alone cannot determine whether an individual was a problem gambler, but tracking data suggested that compared to the non-heavy wagerers, the heavier wagerers tended to spend more time (LaBrie, Kaplan, LaPlante, Nelson, and Shaffer, 2008; LaBrie, LaPlante, Nelson, Schumann, and Shaffer, 2007), and that their activity levels were sustained or increased over time (LaPlante, Schumann, LaBrie, and Shaffer, 2008). Other factors that might indicate that a patron might have a gambling problem could be the duration of play, or the seeking of further funds (Schellinck and Schrans, 2004). Such indicators might be used to by gaming providers to determine which patrons might need assistance. However, some other tendencies of problem gamblers might cause problems. There are indications that problem gamblers play multiple electronic gaming machines at the same time (Delfabbro, Osborn, Nevile, Skelt, and McMillen, 2007; Schellinck and Schrans, 2004). Hence it is likely that it will be difficult to track problem gamblers, and that tracking statistics are likely to be underestimates of a problem gamblers' actual gambling behaviour. Nevertheless if a consumer has a problem, the technology to monitor and inform consumer behaviour is under development. A variety of forms of decisional support have been considered and trialled upon people using electronic gambling devices:

1) Time management advice that informs players as to the passage of time (Ladouceur and Sévigny, 2009).
2) Funds management advice informs players as to the amounts of money wagered, lost or won (Ladouceur and Sévigny, 2009).
3) Precommittment systems seek to encourage players to make decisions as to the amount of time or money they will spend before a gambling session (Broda, LaPlante, Nelson, LaBrie, Bosworth, and Shaffer, 2008; Nelson, LaPlante, Peller, Schumann, LaBrie, and Shaffer, 2008; Nower and Blaszczynski, 2010; Schellinck and Schrans, 2007).
4) Self-barring systems can also be imposed on electronic systems. Where players find they have problems limiting their play, it is possible for them to implement self-barring (Schellinck and Schrans, 2007), and block the player's subsequent attempts to access electronic gambling.
5) Educational advice seeks to counter the irrational cognitions experienced by some gamblers. There are suggestions that this may be useful. The provision of online warnings targetting irrational cognitions appears to correct irrational beliefs and has influenced behaviour both in the laboratory (Floyd, Whelan, and Meyers, 2006) and at the gaming venue (Gainsbury, and Blaszczynski, 2010).

CONCLUSION

The electronic provision of products places a wider variety of services within a consumer's reach. Some of these services (e.g. tobacco advertising, access to pornography, and gambling) challenge a jurisdiction's ability to control content. Recommender technologies serve as personalised shop assistants to convert browsers to buyers, and enhance customer loyalty. Such technologies have outstripped consumer protection methods. A variety of consumer protection methods are under development, but where providers operate on the fringes of respectability, the only inducements to implement consumer protection measures would appear to be attempts to increase consumer confidence.

ACKNOWLEDGMENTS

The authors would like to acknowledge funding support from Gambling Research Australia (Tender No 119/06).

REFERENCES

Aalto, L. Göthlin, N., Korhonen, J., and Ojala, T. (2004). *Bluetooth and WAP push based location-aware mobile advertising system.* In MobiSys '04: Proceedings of the 2nd international conference on Mobile systems, applications, and services (2004), pp. 49-58.

Acquisti, A, and Gross, R. (2006). Imagined communities: Awareness, information sharing, and privacy on the Facebook. *Lecture Notes in Computer Science, 4258,* 36-58.

Ali, K., and van Stam, W. (2004). TiVO: Making show recommendations using a distributed collaborative filtering architecture. Proceedings of KDD'04, Seattle Washington, USA, August 22-25, 2004.

Ang, L., Dubelaar, C., and Lee, B-C. (2001). To trust or not to trust? A model of Internet trust from the customer's point of view. *e-Everything: e-Commerce, e-Government, e-Household, e-Democracy,* 14th Bled Electronic Commerce Conference. Bled, Slovenia, June 25 - 26, 2001

Ba, S., and Pavlou, P.A. (2002). Evidence of the effect of trust building technology in electronic markets: Price premiums and buyer behavior. *MIS Quarterly, 26*(3), 243-268.

Beldad, A., de Jong, M., and Steehouder, M. (2010). How shall I trust the faceless and the intangible? A literature review on the antecedents of online trust. *Computers in Human Behavior, 26,* 857-869.

Blaszczynski, A., Ladouceur, R., Nower, L., and Shaffer, H. (2008). Informed choice and gambling: Principles for consumer protection. *The Journal of Gambling Business and Economics, 2*(1), 103-118.

Blaszczynski, A., Ladouceur, R., and Shaffer, H. (2004). A science-based framework for responsible gambling: The Reno model. *Journal of Gambling Studies, 20,* 301-317.

Boyd, J. (2003). The rhetorical construction of trust. *Online Communication Theory, 13* (4), 392-410.

Boyera, S. (2006). The mobile web to bridge the digital divide. [downloaded 13th May 2010, from http://www-mit.w3.org/2006/12/digital_divide/IST-africa-final.pdf]

Broda, A., LaPante, D.A., Nelson, S.E., LaBrie, R.A., Bosworth, L.B., and Shaffer, H.J. (2008). Virtual harm reduction efforts for Internet gambling: Effects of deposit limits on actual Internet sports gambling behavior. *Harm Reduction Journal, 5,* 27-36.

Chau, A.W., and Phillips, J.G. (1995). Effects of perceived control upon wagering and attributions in computer Blackjack. *Journal of General Psychology, 122*(3), 253-269.

Chau, A.W.L., Phillips, J.G., and Von Baggo, K. (2000). Departures from sensible play in computer Blackjack. *Journal of General Psychology, 127,* 426-438.

Chen, Y-F. (2008). Herd behavior in purchasing books online. *Computers in Human Behavior, 24,* 1977-1992.

Christen, P. (2009). Geocode matching and privacy preservation. *Lecture Notes in Computer Science, 5456,* 7-24.

Debatin, B., Lovejoy, J.P., Horn, A-K., Hughes, B.N. (2009). Facebook and online privacy: Attitudes, behaviors, and unintended consequences. *Journal of Computer-Mediated Communication, 15,* 83-108.

Delfabbro, P., Osborn, A., Nevile, M., Skelt, L., and McMillen, J. (2007). *Identifying Problem Gamblers in Gambling Venues.* Report commissioned for the Ministerial Council on Gambling, Australia.

Dow, K., Serenko, A., Turel, O., and Wong, J. (2006). Antecedents and consequences of user satisfaction with e-mail systems. *International Journal of e-Collaboration, 2*(2), 46-64.

Eadington, W.R. (2004). The future of online gambling in the United States and elsewhere. *Journal of Public Policy and Marketing, 23*(2), 214-219.

Ellison, N.B., Steinfield, C., and Lampe, C. (2007). The benefits of Facebook "friends:" Social capital and college students' use of online social network sites. *Journal of Computer-Mediated Communication, 12*(4), 1143-1168.

Finn, M. (2005). Gaming goes mobile: Issues and implications. *Australian Journal of Emerging Technologies and Society, 3*(1), 31-42.

Floyd, K., Whelan, J.P., and Meyers, A.W. (2006). Use of warning message to modify gambling beliefs and behavior in a laboratory investigation. *Psychology of Addictive Behaviors, 20*(1), 69-74.

Fogel, J., and Nehmad, E. (2009). Internet social network communities: Risk taking, trust, and privacy concerns. *Computers in Human Behavior, 25,* 153-160.

Gainsbury, S., and Blaszczynski, A. (2010). The appropriateness of using laboratories and student participants in gambling research. *Journal of Gambling Studies.* DOI: 10.1007/s10899-010-9190-4.

Gefen D. (2002). Reflections on the dimensions of trust and trustworthiness among online consumers. *The DATA BASE for Advances in Information Systems, 33*(3), 38-53.

George, J.F. (2002). Influences on the intent to make internet purchases. *Internet Research: Electronic Networking Applications and Policy, 12,* 165-180.

Giaglis, G.M., and Lekakos, G. (2006). Improving the prediction accuracy of recommendation algorithms: Approaches anchored on human factors. *Interacting with Computers, 18* (3), 410-431.

Hinze, A., and Quan, Q. (2009). Trust and location-based recommendations for tourism. *Lecture Notes in Computer Science, 5870,* 414-422.

Horst, M., Kuttschreuter, M., and Gutteling, J.M. (2007). Perceived usefulness, personal experiences, risk perception and trust as determinants of adoption of e-government services in The Netherlands. *Computers in Human Behavior, 23,* 1838-1852.

Hrywna, M., Delnevo, C.D., and Lewis, M.J. (2007). Adult recall of tobacco advertising on the internet. *Nicotine and Tobacco Research, 9*(11), 1103-1107.

Hu, R., and Pu, P. (2010). A study on user perception of personality-based recommender systems. *Lecture Notes in Computer Science, 6075*, 291-302.

Ipsos Insight Marketing Research Consultancy: Online video and social networking websites set to drive the evolution of tomorrow's digital lifestyle. Retrieved November, 2010 from http://www.ipsosinsight.com.

Jarvenpaa, S.L., Tractinsky, N., and Vitale, M. (2000). Consumer trust in an internet store. *Information Technology and Management, 1,* 45-71.

Kim, Y.S., Yum, B-J., Song, J., and Kim, S.M. (2005). Development of a recommender system based on navigational and behavioral patterns of customers in e-commerce sites. *Expert Systems with Applications, 28*, 381-393.

Kraut, R.E., Sunder, S., Telang, R., and Morris, J. (2005). Pricing electronic mail to solve the problem of spam. *Human Computer Interaction, 20*, 195-223.

LaBrie, R.A., Kaplan, S.A., LaPlante, D.A., Nelson, S.E., and Shaffer, H.J. (2008). Inside the virtual casino: A prospective longitudinal study of actual Internet casino gambling. *European Journal of Public Health, 18*(4), 410-416.

LaBrie, R.A., LaPlante, D.A., Nelson, S.E., Schumann, A., and Shaffer, H.J. (2007). Assessing the playing field: A prospective longitudinal study of Internet sports gambling behavior. *Journal of Gambling Studies, 23*, 347-362.

Ladouceur, R., and Sévigny, S. (2009). Electronic gambling machines: Influence of a clock, a cash display, and a precommitment on gambling time. *Journal of Gambling Issues, 23*, 31-41.

Lam, S.K., Frankowski, D., and Riedl, J. (2006). Do you trust your recommendations? An exploration of security and privacy issues in recommender systems. *Lecture Notes in Computer Science, 3995*, 14-29.

LaPlante, D.A., Kleschinsky, J.H., LaBrie, R.A., Nelson, S.E., and Shaffer, H.J. (2009). Sitting at the virtual poker table: A prospective epidemiological study of actual Internet poker gambling behavior. *Computers in Human Behavior, 25*, 711-717.

LaPlante, D.A., Schumann, A., LaBrie, R.A., and Shaffer, H.J. (2008). Population trends in Internet sports gambling. *Computers in Human Behavior, 24*, 2399-2414.

Laughlin, A. (2008). Unpublished Honours thesis, Monash University.

Lenhart, A. (2000). Who's not online: 57 percent of those without internet access say they do not plan to log on. *Pew Internet and American Life Project.* Accessed at: www.pewinternet.org, 24th Feb., 2009.

Leskovec, J., Adamic, L.A., and Huberman, B.A. (2007). The dynamics of viral marketing. *ACM Transactions on the Web, 1*(1), 1-39.

Lok, K. (2008). Unpublished Honours thesis, Monash University.

Lewis, K., Kaufman, J., and Christakis, N. (2008). The taste for privacy: An analysis of college student privacy settings in an online social network. *Journal of Computer-Mediated Communication, 14,* 79-100.

Mahatanankoon, P., Wen, H.J., and Lim, B. (2005). Consumer-based m-commerce: Exploring consumer perception of mobile applications. *Computer Standards and Interfaces, 27,*

McManus, P., and Scornavacca, E. (2005). *Mobile marketing: Killer application or new hype?* Paper presented at ICMB 2005. International Conference on Mobile Business.

McSherry, D. (2002). Diversity-conscious retrieval. *Lecture Notes in Artificial Intelligence, 2416,* 219-233.

McSherry, D. (2005). Explanation in recommender systems. *Artificial Intelligence Review, 24,* 179-197.

Mehta, B., and Nejdl, W. (2009). Unsupervised strategies for shilling detection and robust collaborative filtering. *User Modeling and User-Adapted Interaction, 19,* 65–97.

Milgram, S. (1967). The small world problem. *Psychology Today, 1*(61), 56-58.

Min, S-H., and Han, I. (2005). Detection of the customer time-variant pattern for improving recommender systems. *Expert Systems with Applications, 28,* 189-199.

Monaghan, S. (2009). Responsible gambling strategies for internet gambling: The theoretical and empirical base of using pop-up messages to encourage self-awareness. *Computers in Human Behavior, 25,* 202-207.

Montaner, M., Lopez, B., and De La Rosa, J. L. (2003). A taxonomy of recommender agents on the internet. *Artificial Intelligence Review, 19,* 285-330.

Nelson, S.E., LaPlante, D.A., Peller, A.J., Schumann, A., LaBrie, R.A., and Shaffer, H.J. (2008). Real limits in the virtual world: Self-limiting behavior of internet gamblers. *Journal of Gambling Studies, 24,* 463-477.

Neuburger, J.D (2009).. *U.S. Supreme Court (finally) kills online age verification law.* Mediashift. January 29. Available at: *http://www.pbs.*

org/mediashift/2009/01/us-supreme-court-finally-kills-online-age-verification-law029.html. Accessed: 30/4/09

Nielsen, J. (2000) Designing web usability: The practice of simplicity. Indianapolis: New Riders Publishing.

Nower, L., and Blaszczynski, A. (2010). Gambling motivations, money-limiting strategies, and precommitment preferences of problem versus non-problem gamblers. *Journal of Gambling Studies, 26*(3), 361-372.

O'Hare, M.A., Phillips, J., and Moss, S. (2005). *The effects of time-stress, risk level and deductive logic ability on decision making in dynamic environments.* Paper presented at the 32nd conference of the Australasian Experimental Psychology Society, Melbourne, April 2005.

O'Hare, M., Phillips, J.G., and Moss, S. (2009). The effect of contextual and personal factors on the use of recommenders in e-Markets. *The Ergonomics Open Journal, 2*, 207-216

Parasuraman, R., and Riley, V. (1997). Humans and automation: Use, misuse, disuse, abuse. *Human Factors, 39*, 230–253.

Park, D-H., and Lee, J. (2008). eWOM overload and its effect on consumer behavioral intention depending on consumer involvement. *Electronic Commerce Research and Applications, 7*, 386-398.

Perugini, S., Gonçalves, M.A., and Fox, E.A. (2004). Recommender systems research: A connection-centric survey. *Journal of Intelligent Information Systems, 23*(2), 107-143.

Phillips, J. G. and Amrhein, P. C. (1989). Factors influencing wagering in simulated Blackjack. *Journal of Gambling Behavior, 5*(2), 99-111.

Phillips, J.G., and Ogeil, R.P. (2007). Alcohol consumption and computer blackjack. *Journal of General Psychology, 134*(3), 333-353.

Phillips, J.G., Ostojic, P., and Blaszczynski, A. (in press). Mobile phones and inappropriate content. In M.C. Barnes and N.P. Meyers (Eds.) Mobile Phones: Technology, Networks and User Issues. New York: Nova Science Publishers.

Piyasena, I.W.G., and Chan, H.A. (2008). Bridging the interaction barrier with mobile phones by recommending content. IEEE CCNC 2008.

Preece, J.J. (2010). I persuade, they persuade, it persuades! *Lecture Notes in Computer Science, 6137*, 2-3.

Ramakrishnan, N., Keller, B.J., Mirza, B.J., Grama, A.Y., and Karypis, G. (2001). Privacy risks in recommender systems. *IEEE Internet Computing, Nov/Dec*, 54-62.

Resnick, P., and Varian, H.R. (1997). Recommender systems. *Communications of the ACM, 40*(3), 56-58.

Resnick, P., and Zeckhauser, R. (2002). Trust among strangers in internet transactions: Empirical analysis of eBAY's reputation system. The Economics of the Internet and E-Commerce. Michael R. Baye, (Ed.). Volume 11 of Advances in Applied Microeconomics. Amsterdam, Elsevier Science. pp. 127-157.

Saling, L.L. and Phillips, J.G. (2010). The manifestation of neuroticism in the use of information and communication technology. In R.G. Jackson (Ed.), *The Psychology of Neuroticism and Shame* (pp. 59-83). New York: Nova Science Publishers

Schafer, J.B., Konstan, J.A., and Riedl, J. (2001). E-commerce recommendation applications. *Data Mining and Knowledge Discovery, 5*, 115-153.

Schellinck, T. and Schrans, T. (2004). Identifying problem gamblers at the gambling venue: Finding combinations of high confidence indicators. Gambling Research,16, 8-24.

Schellinck, T., and Schrans, T. (2007). VLT Player Tracking System. Report for the Nova Scotia Gaming Corporation Responsible Gaming Research Device Project.

Sévigny, S., Cloutier, M., Pelletier, M-F., and Ladouceur, R. (2005). Internet gambling: Misleading payout rates during the "demo" period. *Computers in Human Behavior, 21*, 153-158.

Shaffer, H.J., Peller, A.J., LaPlante, D.A., Nelson, S.E., and LaBrie, R.A. (2010). Toward a paradigm shift in Internet gambling research: From opinion and self-report to actual behavior. *Addiction Research and Theory, 18*(3), 270-283.

Suh, B., and Han, I. (2002). Effect of trust on consumer acceptance of internet banking. *Electronic Commerce Research and Applications, 1,* 247-263.

Taleb, N.N. (2007). *The Black Swan: The impact of the highly improbable.* London: Penguin Books.

Thorp, E. (1966). *Beat the Dealer.* New York: Vintage.

Tractinsky, N., Katz, A.S., and Ikar D. (2000). What is beautiful is usable. *Interacting with Computers, 13*, 127-145.

Wang, Y.D., and Emurian, H.H. (2005). An overview of online trust: Concepts, elements and implications. *Computers in Human Behavior, 21,* 105-125.

Wang, H., Lee, M.K.O., and Wang, C. (1998). Consumer privacy concerns about internet marketing. *Communications of the ACM, 41,* 63-70.

Whittaker, S., Bellotti, V., and Moody, P (2005). Introduction to the special issue on revisiting and reinventing email. *Human Computer Interaction, 20*, 1-9.

Yang, W-S., Cheng, H-C., and Dia, J-B. (2008). A location-aware recomender system for mobile shopping environments. *Expert Systems with Applications, 34*, 437-445.

Yuan, S.-T., and Tsao, Y. W. (2003). A recommendation mechanism for contextualized mobile advertising. *Expert Systems with Applications, 24*(4), 399-414.

In: Advertising
Editor: Evelyn P. Mann

ISBN 978-1-61324-679-5
© 2012 Nova Science Publishers, Inc.

Chapter 2

THE *LIPDUB* AS A TRENDY WAY OF CORPORATE COMMUNICATION: IMPLICATIONS FOR INSTITUTIONS

Montserrat Díaz-Méndez[*]
University of Extremadura, Spain

ABSTRACT

Lately we are seeing how different kinds of institutions are uploading on the Internet a sort of video clip recorded by a group of people who lip sync to a song, act and dance while the camera follows them through the facilities of the institution they belong to: these are the more and more popular *lipdub* videos. This new communication practice has introduced an important change in the way of approaching institutional communication. The *lipdub* embraces a high component of creativity that allows institutions to showcase a different perspective of themselves which influences the corporate image to a large extent. However, this influence may become also a double edged sword if the performance is not professionally done considering the institution culture and philosophy. That is, although at first sight the *lipdub* seems to be an effective, informal, creative and even funny way of promoting an institution it can cause a serious damage difficult to make up. Private and public companies, Universities, Student Residences and other institutions are taking advantage from this trendy communication tool with the aim of

---

[*] E-mail: mdmendez@unex.es.

enhancing their image and meantime attracting new clients, students or potential employees. In this work we look into the *lipdub* concept, explain its effects on corporate image, assess its value for institutions from a communication perspective by analysing consequences for them and, finally, we suggest a practical guide to perform a successful *lipdub* when advisable. Illustrative examples will be used along the content analysis.

Keywords: institutional communication, corporate image, communication trends, lipdub.

INTRODUCTION

At present there is no doubt that corporate image is a key factor for any organization survival and success. Real competition is in consumer's mind, in this sense, the transmission of ideas, sensations and other intangibles turns out to be crucial for any organization. For this reason, institutional communication (IC) importance in strategic planning is increasing more and more. IC is a strategic communication function that seeks to build mutually beneficial relationships between the organization and its different stakeholders by means of developing a favourable corporate image and reputation of the institution.

Traditionally, organization management and development considered communication issues as of second order category since other subjects of a pure economic and financial nature represented the core of any business. Communication was not professionalized. But this context changed with the Internet boom and organizations started to focus on other aspects more intangible in order to make their organizations stand out from the rest of competitors. It was even considered to be the most important activity of an organization (Costa, 1999). Different communication tactics are being used today to achieve organizational strategic goals: brand design, advertising campaigns, sponsorships, public relations, etc. Regarding this, professionals of communication have to be updated as for the opportunities the new technologies and society and market trends provide them. One of the latest developments on IC activities is the so called *lipdub*. The *lipdub* is a sort of video clip recorded by a group of people who lip sync to a song, act and dance while the camera follows them through the facilities of the institution they belong to. It is an informal way to showcase a different perspective of themselves. The *lipdub* shows the facilities, staff and location of the institution and at the same time it conveys different intangible aspects of itself: working atmosphere, culture, indicators of its service quality (showing satisfaction, facilities and activities), style and so on. However, these possibilities the *lipdub* can offer may become also a double edged sword if the performance is not professionally done considering the institution culture and philosophy. That is, although at first sight the *lipdub* seems to be an effective, informal, creative and even funny way of promoting an institution it can cause a serious damage difficult to make up. Private companies, universities, student residences, hospitals and other institutions are taking advantage from this trendy communication tool with the aim of enhancing their image and meantime attracting new clients, students or potential employees. In this chapter we look into the *lipdub* concept. In first place, some considerations on corporate image and its elements will be made; secondly, we will tackle the role of new technologies in IC; then the *lipdub* and its implications for the organization will be analysed and, finally, we will propose a *lipdub* performance guide in order to prevent organizations from negative effects due to the use of a wrong approach.

1. SOME CONSIDERATIONS ON CORPORATE IMAGE

It is widely accepted that corporate image constitutes a basic strategic element for organizations. It represents an added value and a managerial competitive factor (Mínguez, 2000) that enables organizations to overcome adverse market conditions. It can also be considered as a filter that influence whether positive or negatively the publics' perceptions about certain decision, mistake or action of a company. This is not new. There are many definitions of corporate image. Martínez (2002:10) defines it as the "result of the perceptions and experiences that people get from the organizations. In some sense, it is the visible part of the corporate culture...it is what people think about the organization...people identify an organization for what they see and hear about it, for the way its employees and managers behave, for its public behavior and for the direct or indirect relations they have with it". According to Dowling (2001: 268) it is "the respect and steem in which it (a company) is held". Mínguez (2000:305) refers to corporate image as "all the meanings a person associates to an organization, that is, the ideas used to describe or remember it". Costa (2001:58) understands that corporate image is the "mental representation in the collective people's imaginary of a group of characteristics and values that act as a stereotype and determine the behavior and opinions of those people". For van Riel and Fombrun (2007:68) it consists of the "interpretations stakeholders make about the company". All these definitions share a common idea: people's mental representation and perception of different signs. It is commonly defined as the perception of the organization's identity by its different publics, considering the organization's identity as the self-portrayal of the institution. Corporate image has a dynamic characteristic. It can be altered according to the organization's strategic goals. To do so an organization can manage certain variables in order to achieve its objectives. However corporate image may also be damaged by some external circumstances out of the organization's control: an accident, a mistake, a formal complaint from a client/association with impact in the media, changes in trends and publics' likings, etc. Thus, the importance and vulnerability of the corporate image lead organizations to have among their personnel qualified professionals of communication, although the top management will always be involved in the building of the corporate image process. With the purpose of managing corporate image it is necessary to point out that it is a result of the interactions of different agents and factors: people, commercial communications (advertising and promotions), public relations, media, press articles, manager's public declarations, sponsorship activities and any other action of institutional communication. A serious mistake in any of these factors may destroy a positive global image.

2. ELEMENTS AFFECTING CORPORATE IMAGE

Corporate image is affected by a huge number of variables interconnected to each other. The fact that it constitutes a complex reality to handle makes it necessary to identify certain areas which enable managers to take some control on its development. Following the contribution of different authors (Van Riel, 1997; Mínguez, 2000; Martínez, 2002) we propose here a classification of the main factors that determine corporate image through the consolidation of the corporate identity. It is important to keep in mind that the image will mostly depend on the publics' perceptions of the factors:

a) Behavior: this refers to the way of behaving and answering of all members of the organization.
b) Visual identity: this embraces aspects as the name, brand, and logotype. All these elements graphically represent the corporate essence.

c) Products: this relates to the fact that the very activity the organization is devoted to will determine its identity to a great extent. For instance, a cigarette factory will never enjoy as good image as a factory devoted to recycling. Products in general have a global own image in consumers' mind. In this sense, an organization needs to start from this general image when working on its own products'.

d) Context: this comes to say that also the geographic context where the organization develop its activity will condition part of its corporate image since physical places have their own image too and synergies will inevitably occur.

e) Culture: shared values of an organization constitute internal integration elements and help to build the corporate identity from a social perspective.

f) Communications: this encompasses those processes, messages and means involved in the information transmission of the organization.

These factors must convey a consistent message (Fombrun and van Riel, 2004). If corporate communications overlap or sound contradictory the image will end up damaged. Experience has demonstrated that it is easier to prevent one's image to result damaged than to try to restore it. Thus, it is advisable that the top management monitors every communication activity the organization is going to undertake. Messages have to be coherent in order to reinforce credibility. A wrong message, the wrong means, the wrong target-audience or the wrong moment may cause serious damage to an organization's image.

Finally, once the corporate identity has been programmed the different publics of the organization will get the messages from it and form a determined image. This image can be the same for all of them or may vary.

3. TRENDS IN CORPORATE COMMUNICATION: THE *LIPDUB*

As corporate image has the ability of being continuously altered (Costa, 2001), organizations need to be updated as for what is going on on corporate image subjects and also they have to strive to innovate. Being the first in thinking up a new way of communicating translates into a very valuable benefit for the organization. In this sense, the new technologies -specially the Web 2.0- are providing organizations with a great deal of choices to develop their image through different concepts: interactivity, modernity, transparency, accessibility, proximity, originality, etc. Some organizations are faster than others in adopting the new trends in communication, most of them related to the new technologies. This new approach of corporate image through new technologies gives rise to the so-called *digital corporate image.* At present, the digital corporate image entails different elements practically within any organizations' reach: web sites, interactive catalogs, newsletters, corporate blogs, podcasts, nanoblogging, presence in social networks, videos publishing in mass participatory video content sites, etc. In this chapter we deal with a communication tool of great novelty among organizations that is being used more and more: the *lipdub.* It can be defined as a one- shot and amateur video clip recorded by a group of people who lip sync to a song, act and dance while the camera follows them through the facilities of the institution they belong to. The *lipdub* concept was coined by one of the founders of the video-sharing website Vimeo, Jakob Lodwick, in 2006, in a video entitled *Lip Dubbing: Endless Dream.* One can read below the video an author's explanation saying: *"I walked around with a song playing in my headphones, and recorded myself singing. When I got home I opened it in iMovie and added an MP3 of the actual song, and synchronized it with my video. Is there a name for this? If not, I suggest 'lip dubbing'."*

Service /video name	URL
Vimeo	http://vimeo.com/
Lip Dubbing: Endless Dream	http://www.vimeo.com/123498

The first *lipdub* as we know it at present came from a group of students from the University of Furtwangen (Germany) in 2008. However it reached its peak of popularity when the students of Communication of the University of Quebec (Canada) uploaded their *lipdub* in the Internet as a response to the University of Furtwangen public calling for new lipdubs. It went soon around the world.

It had a great impact on international media and from that moment on all kinds of organizations tried to copy the idea and create their particular *lipdub*s. Then a battle to be the most remarkable and original one started.

Organization/institution name	URL
University of Furtwangen	http://university*lipdub*.com/videos/
Université du Québec à Montréal (UQAM)	http://www.youtube.com/watch?v=-zcOFN_VBVo

The original University lipdub: University of Furtwangen
The lipdub phenomenon as we know it today came from an initiative of a group of
students from the University of Furtwangen (Germany). They filmed their own lipdub
and then opened up a website where they invited universities from all around the world
to produce their own lipdubs so that they would gather them on the University lipdub
site. At present this site shows more than fifty lipdubs from Universities from all around
the world.
See the videos here: http://universitylipdub.com/response-

The *lipdub* as a way to communicate an institutional message is been used
currently to promote private and public companies, cities, candidacies, student
residences, residences for the elderly, schools, events, universities, etc.

An outstanding experience: The JandB *Lipdub* contest
The famous whisky brand JandB was quick and clever when detecting such a great opportunity to build a strong link between the company and one of its targets, the University students. JandB sponsored an artistic contest in Spain where all universities were invited to participate. The invitation was addressed to students not to the institution itself. A group of six students in charge to direct and perform the *lipdub* could only register in the contest through the social network Kedin. This initiative had a space in Facebook and Youtube where students could follow the development of the contest. The prize for the winner consisted of 3.000 euros and the organization of a big party for the students from the winner University. The JandB *lipdub* contest became a real phenomenon among students from universities of all Spain. The success went beyond all expectations with more than 900.000 visits to the contest website. Twelve universities participated finally. Students had to show they were having fun during the recording of the *lidub* at the time they used and showed different JandB promotional items. This promotional activity run by JandB brand can be considered one of the most successful activities in the world in terms of image creation through the use of the *lipdub*. A whisky brand got to link its own values to the traditional University values. At present alcoholic drinks are experiencing a reputation devaluation and, in general, they need to change society perception… is there a better way to do so than to relate alcohol with high education? However, after seeing all the videos some questions arise: Did these Universities managing boards know their students were using the name of the institution to participate in a contest sponsored by a whisky brand? Did they see the videos before they were uploaded in the Internet? Has the image of any of them been affected?   See the videos here: http://www.youtube.com/user/JBinventivesince1749#p/f/0/wRdvFIPzTg0   A special mention deserves the winner *lipdub* of this contest, the University Centre of Villanueva (Madrid, Spain). This *lipdub* represents a good example of what a good *lipdub* should be. It encompasses most of the formal and technical requirements to get a high quality *lipdub*.   See the winner video: http://www.*lipdub*.eu/blog/university-*lipdub*-with-a-jb-sponsor/#more-1532

It is been widely spread to different areas but the *lipdub* is been especially successful at the University context. The success in this context has led other companies to take advantage of this phenomenon to enhance their image or increase their advertising impact.

4. THE *LIPDUB* IMPLICATIONS FOR THE ORGANIZATION

As most communication activities, the *lipdub* presents some lights and shades. Any organizational communication activity has an effect on the organization's image. The *lipdub* institutional videos have changed the way communication activities are traditionally understood and for that reason its use has to be careful in order not to make serious mistakes. On one hand, the *lipdub* provides the organization with the following benefits:

- It shows a friendly face of the organization. Thus, it tries to get closer to their publics. The fact that the organization's staff gets involved in a project like doing a *lipdub* conveys the image that people are satisfied and happy working for that institution. Society appreciates more and more organizations that are friendly with their employees since there is a greater concern about how important the working environment is for a person to be happy. The *lipdub* definition implies that the participation in it can not be mandatory, that is, the boss can not oblige an employee to participate and pretend he or she enjoys working for that company. Therefore, the different publics understand that the staff of the company that is performing the *lipdub* does really enjoy belonging to that company.
- It is a way to showcase the organization's facilities. Physical evidence is taken into account by different publics of an organization to make up a global image of the organization. Levitt (1981) said that tangible elements help clients to trust in a certain service provider. In general, it is accepted that the tangible environment constitutes a source of value creation and it may encompass the following elements: technological equipments, neat-looking employees, light, colour, textures, furniture material and style, wall decoration, etc. the visualization of all these elements in a *lipdub* will influence the viewer's perception of the company.

- It serves as a motivating activity for the organization's staff. It helps to integrate employees and to foster relationships among them. Having fun together is an effective way to get a closer link to others. The decision to perform a *lipdub* may also be motivated by the wish to promote a good working atmosphere among employees as an activity of "team building" in order to increase productivity.

- It constitutes an opportunity for the organization's managers to remind their employees the organization's philosophy. Before performing the *lipdub* the objectives it pursues must be clear for all participants -usually a great part of the staff. The objectives need to be established by the managing board and will be focused on transmitting as clear as possible the organization's philosophy. "Lies are not profitable and end up damaging even the most solid image" (Álvarez and Caballero, 1997:119).

- If the *lipdub* is successful it will be spread over the Internet through e-mail, blogs, online social networks, and other Internet services. Thus increasing outstandingly corporate knowledge.

- In some cases the *lipdub* can also serve as a "window" to advertise other brands of the organization or related products. It is more and more common to see small advertisements at the bottom of the *lipdub* videos. For example, it is easy to find some master courses or students residences advertised in some Universities' *lipdub*s.

As a result of these benefits potential clients may become actual clients, potential employees may feel encouraged to apply for a job in that company, general society may generate positive word of mouth, the media may talk about the company for free and in an independent way and all this positive effects may motivate the staff to increase productivity at work. See some examples of companies' lipdub here:

Organization name	URL
Adidas	http://www.youtube.com/watch?v=0p6m3vZjXtoandfeature=player_embedded
Vueling Airlines	http://www.youtube.com/watch?v=WyJDimcdbLs

On the other hand, a wrong understanding of what a *lipdub* is may cause some negative effects for an institution image. It is important to be careful when deciding to undertake this apparently simple and informal project like doing a *lipdub*.

> Vueling Airlines Lipdup: an example of good performance.
> The Spanish low-fare airline, Vueling, merged with Iberia, used this *lipdub* as a Christmas greeting. The managers made the decision to carry out this kind of video due to several factors: (1) it was original and different by that time, Vueling was the first Spanish company in doing a *lipdub*; (2) they had something to show, they were convinced they could fit to was expected from a *lipdub* as a corporate communication instrument; (3) it could be spread over the Internet and be used as a kind of viral marketing video; (4) and finally, the idea turned out to be specially interesting because doing a *lipdub* is quite inexpensive, in a economic crisis period it constitutes a non expensive choice to reinforce corporate image. This video gathers almost all characteristics required to perform a high quality *lipdub*.

The main problem relates to the fact that corporate image can turn out damaged because of the low quality standards of the *lipdub*. We should start by the premise that a *lipdub* is not a high quality video but this should not lead us to think that anything can be a good *lipdub*. Some *lipdub*s are better than others. Specifically, the following factors may represent a source of troubles for an organization:

- The *lipdub* is performed out of the supervision of the top management of the institution. This could be considered the most important factor out of the rest since it gathers to some extent the others' content. A *lipdub* uses the name of an institution therefore it contributes to build its corporate image. Corporate image creation is an executive function; for this reason, the top managers can not distance themselves from the development of the *lipdub* project. A wrong approach may destroy some previous work done. This circumstance takes place especially in the University context. There is not usually a close relationship between students and the institution managers and many times the initiative of doing a *lipdub* comes directly from students. Also, students are not usually concerned with the effects a *lipdub* may have on their university image and they only care about the idea of having fun and uploading the video in the Internet so that their friends can see them acting. And this embraces a risk for Universities. If the *lipdub* conveys different values to those the University is working on, or it shows the facilities the University would never show, or it shows its students do not look to be talentful, or simply, the *lipdub* does not reflect the identity of the University just because the students who have done it are no qualified to do so, in that case, the University "advertised" has got a problem. It is important to note that Internet services like Youtube play a role on University students' mobility. Many students seek information about different possible universities where to study before making a decision, and this kind of services help them a lot since *images speak louder than words* and students prefer to see videos and build their own picture of what their stay there could be like. In short, the *lipdub* performance has to be supervised in order to protect corporate image.

- Lack of appropriate technical means. Although the essence of the *lipdub* consists of its amateur and non professional nature, we insist on the idea that some standards have to be observed. Watching a *lipdub* has to be a comfortable thing for the viewer through image stability and sound quality.

- The *lipdub* is not really such. Some organizations are using the word *lipdub* to launch some kind of promotional video recorded with high-performance equipments. In these cases, the organization may get two different results: people will think whether they do not really know what a *lipdub* is or that they aim to cheat the viewers. Both cases are detrimental for an institution image.

- The reality to show through the *lipdub* is not honestly good to be shown. If the institution aims to show a false image of itself it is better to avoid doing a *lipdub*. It is difficult and unethical to get employees or students or other public involved in a lie.

- People –whether employees or students- do not play well their roles. Even if it a non-professional video, and employees or students are not supposed to be actors there are some standards that need to be fulfil in order to achieve the communication goals. There are no excuses to perform a video uncomfortable to see. In the end, the *lipdub* pursues very important and delicate objectives for the organization and needs to be seriously approached. Viewers may unconsciously relate the quality of the performance of the participants in the *lipdub* with the quality of their professional talent. Image is about perceptions; and, in this sense it is important that the person/team in charge to develop a *lipdub* has some psychology knowledge and have the ability to anticipate the reaction of the viewers.

To finish up this section, it is important to note that *lipdub*'s publics are very demanding when assessing the quality of a *lipdub*. At least they expect it gathers the basic characteristics.

5. A *LIPDUB* PERFORMANCE GUIDE

In order to perform a high quality *lipdub* for an institution we propose here some tips:

1) Having a good idea. In this sense, apart from having an original and creative idea it is important to consider the convenience of doing a *lipdub* for that institution. It is also a prerequisite to know well the characteristics of a *lipdub*: its formal and technical requirements and its communication purposes.

2) Top management acceptance. According to what we said in the previous section, top managers have to be informed of the progress of the process of performing a libdub and they must actively supervise it in order to avoid detrimental mistakes for corporate image.

3) Setting objectives. Since it constitutes a communication instrument it must be planned so as to achieve some communication objectives. What does the institution wants to get by uploading its *lipdub* on the web? A institution may pursue to change its social image, attract potential talented employees, attract students, clients, etc. Even if the main objective of an institution when performing a *lipdub* is to create a team attitude among its employees, the institution must keep in mind that it is also going to generate some other additional effects when people see the video.

4) Outlining the storyboard. Once the objectives are clear the next step consists of designing an outline of what scenes could be included, what the central thread could be, possible characters, clothes, etc.

5) Choose the song. There are different points of view as for what type of music to choose. Classic songs present the big advantage that they never go out of fashion. On the other side, the main advantages of featuring a recent worldwide hit is that, in many cases participants do already know the words and also viewers enjoy watching the *lipdub* in the very moment it is uploaded because of the fact the song is on everyone's lips by that time.

Examples of lipdubs that use classic songs		
Song title	Institution	URL
Classic song: Rama Lama Ding Dong- Rocky Sharpe and the replace	Communication Faculty of the University of Navarra	http://www.youtube.com/watch? v=mI3m0tnVrmg
I want you back- Jackson 5	Boston University	http://www.youtube.com/watch? v=Mw6I51UE1W8

Examples of *lipdub*s that use songs of the moment		
Song title	Institution	URL
I gotta feeling- Black-eyed Peas	Communication Faculty of the University of Quebec at Montreal (UQAM), Canada	http://www.youtube.com/watch? v=-zcOFN_VBVo
If We Ever Meet Again- Timbaland and Katy Perry	Dizengoff Center Tel Aviv, Israel (mall)	http://www.youtube.com/watch? v=74nyKaQ0LBY

As for the use of a song it is important to know the corresponding rules regarding copyright aspects.

6) Design the final storyboard. After the song is chosen the team in charge of directing the *lipdub* has to write the final storyboard defining exhaustively the sequence of scenes: the route, choreographies, timings, and also specific people for determined scenes. The *lipdub* director must keep in mind that the less chaotic the *lipdub* is the greater acceptance it will get. As for the content it is also advisable to avoid political, religious, bad taste or any other controversial messages. The *lipdub* started as a creative and friendly communication instrument and it would be detrimental for this new communication type to use it as a polemical issues protest tool.

7) Choose the main characters. This step implies selecting the rest of people that are playing a role in the *lipdub*. They should represent the image the institution wants to show and also they must commit to take the *lipdub* seriously as a corporate communication activity with certain objectives. Some people may think participating in a *lipdub* is just a matter of having fun; they must know in advance they are

representing an institution. For example: the *lipdub* essence consists of lip synching and audio dubbing of a song, however, there are many *lipdub*s where the actors have not worried about learning the words and they just move their lips without any synchronization with the song. This small detail lowers the quality of the *lipdub*.

8) Appropriate equipment. Although the *lipdub* is not a professional video it requires certain technical standards too. At this point having a professional's advice is very valuable. Here there are some aspects the *lipdub* directors must be aware of:

- The image quality has to be clear.
- The image has to be as stable as possible: the director of the *lipdub* should know there are techniques used to reduce blurring associated with the motion of the camera. With this aim he or she should count on someone who knows these techniques, preferably a professional. Too many movements of the camera may get the viewer tired and dizzy.
- A *lipdub* is a one-shot video.

9) Rehearsals. A good principle to guarantee the *lipdub* success is to learn that improvisation is the exception, not the rule. To get a good outcome it is necessary to repeat several times the *lipdub* before the final shooting. Correcting mistakes and giving advice to the participants will help to improve the quality of the *lipdub*. Thus increasing the probabilities of getting a greater acceptance. As for the rehearsals, some institutions also upload in the Internet some videos which they call the *lipdub making of* and use them as a way to communicate certain messages: fun, professionalism, good working environment, etc. The following are some remarkable examples of *making of* videos due to the relevance of the *lipdub*s and the professionalism of the videos:

Institution	URL
UQAM, Canada	http://www.youtube.com/watch?v=3z1Pr0ayzik
Comm University of Navarra, Spain	http://www.youtube.com/watch?v=24Ppxxbz8GU

10) Filming. At this point most work is already done. If the previous steps have been carefully considered the shooting of the video will turn out

to be an easy task. It may require making several takes. Having a professional in the *lipdub* team is a profitable investment.

11) Editing. This consists basically of assembling images with music, in principle this is not complicated. The *lipdub* editing does not require any selection of shots since it is made only of one shot.

12) Distribution. This is the final step and involves choosing the channels through which the *lipdub* can be watched: e-mail, blogs, intranet, mass participatory video content sites, corporate websites, etc.

CONCLUSION

Organization need more and more to communicate with their publics in an effective way. Conveying the right message in the right way is a task communication professionals are devoted to nowadays. They seek new communication channels as the audiences profiles change. In this sense, the *lipdub* video has arisen as an original and quite effective way to convey a corporate message to different targets.

The *lipdub* is a sort of video clip filmed by a group of people who lip sync to a song, act and dance while the camera follows them through the facilities of the institution they belong to. It is profusely used to promote universities but other institutions are coming out with this idea and are performing their own *lipdub* too. The *lipdub* was first used with a promotional purpose by the students of the German University of Furtwangen but it reached its peak of popularity when the students of Communication of the University of Quebec (Canada) uploaded their *lipdub* in the Internet. From that moment it became a social phenomenon. Many organizations tried to get advantaged of this trendy way to communicate: some by doing their own lipdups, others by organizing and sponsoring *lipdub* contests and others by inserting advertisements in other's *lipdub*s.

There are many benefits the *lipdub* can provide to institutions: it shows a friendly face of the organization, is a way to showcase the organization's facilities, serves as a motivating activity for the organization's staff, constitutes an opportunity for the organization's managers to remind their employees the organization's philosophy and if the *lipdub* is successful it will be spread over the Internet increasing the knowledge of the institution. These positive aspects the libdub offers to an organization can turn into a double edged sword if the presence of any of the following factors occurs: the *lipdub* is performed out of the supervision of the top management of the institution, there is a lack of appropriate technical means, the *lipdub* does not gather its distinctive features, the reality to show through the *lipdub* is not good to be shown or participants do not play well their roles. Among these negative factors the most important one is the first one: the supervision of the top management. If the managers of the organization supervise the *lipdub* process and outcome it can be assured that the corporate values are respected and observed. This also includes the assessment of technical aspects; a bad quality video would convey a negative image of the organization, this is the reason why it is important to have a professional in the *lipdub* team.

With the aim of making the most of an organization's *lipdub* and avoid the potential negative consequences it may cause, a starting guide has been proposed. Thus twelve steps are suggested: (1) having a good idea, (2) top management acceptance, (3) setting objectives, (4) outline the storyboard, (5) choose the song, (6) design the final storyboard, (7) choose the main characters, (8) appropriate equipment, (9) rehearsals, (10) filming, (11) editing and (12) distribution. Observing these steps to the detail will ensure a positive outcome. As it can be deduced through the content of this chapter, doing a good *lipdub* takes a lot of effort. At present, some organizations have experienced a detriment of their image due to the uploading of a bad *lipdub* on the Internet; some, especially Universities, because the institution managers did not even know what their students were carrying out; and others, because the institution could not foresee the effects the *lipdub* could have on the corporate image. There is a popular saying that states that at the beginning of a novelty the most important thing is to "get the first to the market" and later the important thing is just being there. However, let us not forget that *haste makes waste*.

REFERENCES

Álvarez, T. and Caballero, M. (1997). Vendedores de imagen. Los retos de los nuevos gabinetes de comunicación. Madrid: Paidós, Papeles de Comunicación, 18.

Costa, J. (1999). La comunicación en acción. Informe sobre la nueva cultura. Madrid: Paidós. (2001). La imagen corporativa en el siglo XXI. Buenos Aires: La Crujía Ediciones.

Fombrun, C. J. and van Riel, C.B.M. (2004). Fame and fortune: how successful companies build winning reputation. London: Pearson Financial Times.

Grahame R., and Dowling, G. R. (2000). How Journalists Evaluate Corporate Reputations. ANZMAC 2000 Visionary Marketing for the 21st Century: Facing the Challenge.

Islas, O. (2005). De las relaciones públicas a la comunicación estratégica, Revista Latinoamericana de Comunicación Chasqui 89 – March.

Levitt, T. (1981). Marketing Intangible Products and Product Intangibles. *Harvard Business Review.* Vol. 59, 95-102.

Martínez Selva, J. M. (2002). Marketing de servicios profesionales. Para la pequeña y mediana empresa. Madrid: Prentice Hall.

Mínguez Arranz, N. (2000). Un marco conceptual para la comunicación corporativa. Zer Revista de Estudios de Comunicación 8, 303-321.

Van Riel, C. (1997): *Comunicación corporativa.* Madrid: Prentice Hall.

Van Riel, C.B.M and Fombrun C. J., (2007): *Essentials of corporate communication: implementing practices for effective reputation management.* Routledge.

Main URL Consulted:

Kedin: http://blog.kedin.es
Lip Dub: www.lipdub.eu/
University Lipdub: http://university*lipdub*.com/videos
University of Navarra. http://www.unav.es/fcom/lipdub/index.htm
UQAM: http://www.faccom.uqam.ca/Page/default.aspx
Vimeo: www.vimeo.com
Wikipedia: http://en.wikipedia.org/ http://es.wikipedia.org
YouTube: www.youtube.com

In: Advertising
Editor: Evelyn P. Mann

ISBN 978-1-61324-679-5
© 2012 Nova Science Publishers, Inc.

Chapter 3

THE IMPACT OF CONGRUENCY AND TIME PRESSURE DURING SIMULTANEOUS EXPOSURE IN AN IDTV CONTEXT

Katarina Panić[1], Verolien Cauberghe[2] and Patrick De Pelsmacker[3]*

[1]Ghent University - Department of Communication Sciences
Korte Meer 7-9-11, 9000 Ghent, Belgium
[2]Ghent University – Department of Communication Sciences, Korte Meer 7-9-11, 9000 Ghent, Belgium
[3]University of Antwerp – Marketing Department, Stadscampus Kipdorp 61 2000 Antwerp, Belgium

ABSTRACT

In today's cluttered media environment, advertisers are constantly in search for new ways to improve the strength and effectiveness of their advertisements. They are continuously competing for the limited attention resources of consumers, declaring a so called "war for eye balls" (Schiessl et al., 2003). Contrary to the traditional, sequential formats of advertising, new technologies like Interactive Digital Television (IDTV) allow simultaneous exposure to media content and interactive advertising content using on-screen placements, television banners (Cauberghe and

*E-mail: Katarina.Panic@UGent.be, Tel: +32 9 264 68 81.

De Pelsmacker, 2008) or split-screen advertising (Chowdhury et al., 2007). Therefore, it is important to understand which factors determine viewer attention in today's cluttered and increasingly complex media environment.

In this study, viewers are simultaneously exposed to both an interactive advertisement and a program context using IDTV technology. By doing so, they are forced to divide their attention between both information sources. This may lead to cognitive interference and consequently to less attention devoted to the advertisement. Using eye tracking, we study the role of program environment, more specifically how a thematically (in)congruent program affects both visual attention to an interactive ad and involvement with the ad message. Also, we investigate how congruence moderates the effect of cognitive load resulting from time pressure, while interacting with the interactive ad.

Results show that when viewers are simultaneously exposed to a congruent context (i.e. the program and the interactive advertisement are thematically congruent), they devote more visual attention to the ad and jump more between the ad and the program than when the ad is processed in an incongruent context. Viewers are hindered and distracted by the fact that the information in the ad merges with the program context, therefore needing more time to disentangle both. Processing the information in an incongruent context, on the other hand, is less interfering and thus requires less time. Also, time pressure significantly reduces ad viewing time in the congruent context, while it does not affect viewing time in the incongruent situation. Further, results show a higher involvement with the ad message in the incongruent that in the congruent condition but increasing time pressure, on the other hand, does not appear to affect message involvement.

INTRODUCTION

Contrary to the traditional sequential formats of advertising, people are nowadays increasingly exposed to media and advertising content simultaneously (e.g., pop ups, banner advertisements, streaming video on web pages, etc.). This phenomenon is not restricted to the Internet. New technologies like Interactive Digital Television (IDTV) aim to combine the interactivity of the internet with the broadcasting of traditional television. This allows simultaneous exposure to media content and interactive advertising content, using for example on-screen placements of television banners (Cauberghe and De Pelsmacker, 2008) or split-screen advertising (Chowdhury et al., 2007). Today, consumers are exposed to an increasing amount of advertising content (Lee and Lee, 2007) and marketers are continuously competing for the limited attention resources of consumers (the "war for eye balls", Schiessl et al., 2003). Therefore, it is important to understand which factors determine viewer attention in today's cluttered and increasingly complex media environment.

Using eye tracking, the present paper studies the impact of program congruency and time pressure on the attention paid to an interactive (or telescopic) television ad shown simultaneously with a program context. Compared with a traditional ad, this format is more complex since viewers are forced to divide their attention between both information sources. This can lead to an interference effect, defined as *"the process by which our ability to recollect information is hindered by our exposure to some other information"* (Kumar, 2000, p.155). Interference effects are usually found when people are exposed to different stimuli with similar verbal (e.g. messages, brand names) or contextual (e.g. colors, sounds) elements, but recent research has established that the thematic congruency of stimuli can also moderate this interference effect (Furnham et al., 2002; Cauberghe et al., 2009). In today's fast-paced world where information is continuously received, people are often in a hurry to process ads to be able to continue watching the television program. The issue of responding to time pressure in a viewing context is therefore highly important (Hahn et al., 1992). Time pressure creates a cognitive discrepancy between the time available and the time required to perform a given task (Hornik, 1984). When people are subjected to time pressure, it may affect their cognitive load (Paas and van Merriënboer, 1994). Consequently, time pressure may diminish the attention devoted to the ad. The question is to what extent program congruency moderates this effect of time pressure.

The main contribution of this chapter is to investigate these interference effects on attention paid to an interactive ad during the simultaneous exposure to this ad and a media context. By means of eye tracking, we study how a thematically congruent or incongruent program affects visual attention and how this congruency moderates the effect of cognitive load resulting from time pressure while interacting with the interactive ad.

CONCEPTUAL FRAMEWORK AND HYPOTHESES

When simultaneously exposed to an (interactive) ad and a TV program (or a website and a banner or streaming video), viewers usually divide their attention between both information sources in order to understand and process the information. This may lead to a cognitive interference effect. According to Furnham and colleagues (2002), this interference effect is more substantial when the advertisement and the program context are thematically congruent than when they are incongruent. When an ad is placed in a program of similar content, elements of the program and the ad merge together in a phenomenon known as 'meltdown'. As a result, recall performance declines (Furnham et al., 2002). Congruent stimuli compete for attention and therefore may interfere with each other, thus inhibiting the retrieval of separate information items (Kumar, 2000). This can be harmful for the effectiveness of the ad. On the other hand, researchers also observed positive advertising effects when exposing people to thematically congruent context information. According to the cognitive priming theory, an ad that is preceded by a program of similar content or nature will be remembered better than when the ad is placed in a program with wholly dissimilar content (Sanbonmatsu and Fazio, 1991). This priming can lead to increased attention and increased information processing (Herr, 1989). Congruent context information may indeed cognitively prime the embedded advertisement. Either way, following the incongruence theory (e.g., Mandler, 1982), we expect that distinguishing between elements of an ad and a program is more difficult (and demands more mental effort) when these are congruent than when they are incongruent. Consequently, viewers will need more time to process this cognitive difficulty caused by the interference and the battle for attention, leading to a longer ad viewing time in the congruent condition than in the incongruent condition. The assumption that visual attention is a good proxy for mental attention has been proven correct in the past (Gentry, 2007). Also, we expect that, if viewers want to process the ad in a congruent program situation, they may need to switch their attention more from program to ad and back to 'neutralize' the confusion between both, and avoid the meltdown effect. In other words, a good understanding of the ad will force viewers who are exposed to a congruent context to switch their gaze more often between the ad and the program, i.e. jump from ad to program and back. This gaze switching is less needed or activated in an incongruent context because of the attention-stimulating contrast between the program and the ad. Hence:

   H1a: When the content of the program is thematically congruent with the content of the interactive ad, viewers will devote more attention (measured by total viewing time of the ad) to the interactive ad than when the program content is incongruent

H1b: When the content of the program is thematically congruent with the content of the interactive ad, viewers will divide their attention (measured by the amount of gaze jumps per second) more between the interactive information and the program than when the program content is incongruent

Further, we hypothesize that time pressure during the simultaneous viewing experience will have an impact on the viewing behavior. Since respondents already experience a cognitively demanding situation (simultaneous exposure), and since humans have a limited capacity to process information (Bolls et al., 1996; Lang et al., 1996; Lang, 2000), we expect that information processing will decrease when the total viewing time is limited and viewers are pressed for time. Previous research has shown that time pressure reduces mental capacity (Wegner et al., 1993, Maule and Svenson, 1993) and increases cognitive load *("the load that performing a particular task imposes on the learner's cognitive system"*, Paas and Van Merrienboer, 1994, p.353). The perception that time is restricted reduces cognitive capacity because the awareness of time pressure demands that cognitive resources are allocated to cope with the limited time and to monitor the time available (Maule and Svenson, 1993; Ordonez and Benson, 1997). Also, increasing time pressure may lead to increased task-irrelevant thoughts like worrisome thoughts. These thoughts may interfere with attention paid to relevant information, utilizing cognitive resources that would otherwise be available for task performance (Eysenck and Calvo, 1992; Coy, 1997). In sum, time pressure increases cognitive load and limits the capacity to process information. Because of greater interference and the resulting meltdown, thematic congruence is expected to increase cognitive load. Therefore, viewers will need to devote more mental effort to processing the interactive ad information. Consequently, we expect viewers in a congruent context to devote significantly less time viewing the ad under time pressure than without time pressure. If, on the other hand, the content of the ad and the program are incongruent, we expect viewers to be able to keep elements from both information resources separate, hereby reducing cognitive load. Consequently, we expect that the impact of time pressure on viewing behavior is weaker in an incongruent ad/program context than in a congruent context:

H2: Time pressure reduces ad viewing time more when the content of the program is thematically congruent with the ad than when the program and the ad are incongruent.

Since viewers are less distracted by the interfering program content in the incongruent condition, this allows them to better focus their attention on the ad than in the congruent condition. Therefore, we expect that they will be able to process the information in the ad better and more thorough. As a consequence, we hypothesize that involvement with the advertising message will be higher in the incongruent condition than in the congruent one:

H3a: Involvement with the message will be higher in the thematically incongruent than in the congruent program condition.

Previous research has already shown that when time pressure is high, individuals are unable to utilize the available cognitive resources to systematically analyze the message arguments. In contrast, the amount of attention allocated to the message is not impeded when individuals are under low or no time pressure (MacInnis, Moorman, and Jaworski, 1991). Hence, respondents may apply the available cognitive resources to better process and understand the message arguments. Thus we expect the involvement with the message to be lower in the condition with time pressure than without time pressure:

H3b: Increasing time pressure leads to lower involvement with the message.

METHOD

Procedure

The experiment was set in an interactive television context, using a telescopic ad which consists of a "30-second TV ad with a call-to-action button with clickable content or micro sites featuring individual still screens providing additional product information" (Bellman and Varan, 2004, p.2). This new advertising format enables to show program and advertising content simultaneously. When the viewer clicks on the call-to-action, he/she leaves the linear broadcast stream to enter a Dedicated Advertising Location (DAL). There, the viewer can navigate through the additional information. To avoid that people would miss part of their program while navigating in the DAL, the advertising format shows the ongoing broadcast content in the right upper corner, using picture-in-picture technology. Several studies have demonstrated the effectiveness of this new advertising format (Chang and Thorson, 2004; Bellman and Varan, 2004; Reading et al., 2006). The experiment was conducted in a living room setting. Participants were individually asked to take place in front of an eye tracker, which closely resembled to a television screen. First, participants watched a 10 minute during sequence of a television program, followed by a traditional 30-second public service announcement (PSA) that contained a call-to-action button and a voice-over requesting participants to press the red button.

After responding to the call-to-action, an interactive part displaying clickable information appeared. From this moment on, the participants' viewing behavior was registered by the eye tracker. While participants browsed through the interactive information, the ongoing television program was shown in the right upper corner (filling one quarter of the screen, see figure 1). After the experiment, subjects were asked to fill out a standardized questionnaire.

Stimuli and Participants

A between-subjects 2 (program context: congruent vs. incongruent) × 2 (time constraint vs. no time constraint) factorial design was used. For the 30-second ad, we used a PSA stressing the dangers of incorrect or needless use of antibiotics. The interactive DAL contained additional information about the use of antibiotics. The ad and the DAL were identical across conditions. Simultaneous with the interactive information, the audiovisual program context appeared in the right upper corner of the screen. In the thematically incongruent condition, a sequence from the movie 'Taxi' was shown. The message of the ad ('the correct use of antibiotics') was thematically incongruent with the movie sequence showing two police officers trying to outsmart some criminals.

For the congruent condition, we select a sequence featuring a doctor explaining a medical treatment to a patient and the patient receiving medication in a hospital. The use of medicine to counter a virus and the medical context of the program sequence are both thematically congruent with the ad message.

We manipulated time pressure by either constraining the time available to navigate through the additional interactive information to 120 seconds or by giving subjects as much time as they wanted. In the time-pressure condition, participants were told to go through the information as quickly as possible. To avoid that they would just quickly scroll through the information, they were told that they had to process the information thoroughly within the given time, because afterwards they would be tested on how much they had remembered. To ensure that subjects felt time pressure, they were given verbal warnings by the experimenter when 60 seconds remained and again when 30 seconds remained. In addition, a small digital count-down timer was used to announce the end of the 2 minute time period.

A pretest was used to check if the (in)congruence of the advertisement and the program manipulation was successful. Sixteen randomly selected respondents (20% male, average age = 23) were either exposed to the congruent or the incongruent context.

Afterwards, they had to evaluate the ad and context as either thematically congruent or incongruent. Fourteen out of 16 respondents answered all the (in)congruency questions correctly.

In addition, the pretest was used to determine the appropriate length of the time constraint. We timed subjects on navigating through the information in the DAL, after they were given the instruction to navigate as fast, but as thoroughly as possible through it.

The average time spent in the DAL was 156 seconds with a standard deviation of 35 seconds. In line with Benson and Svenson (1993), the time constraint was determined as the mean execution time minus one standard deviation. Therefore, the time constraint used in the experiment is 120 seconds.

The respondents were randomly assigned across the different conditions. In total, 136 subjects participated in the study, 28% of whom were male. The average age of the respondents was 22 years (range 20 to 27 years).

Measures

Involvement was measured using Cox and Cox's (2001) six-item five-point Likert scale ($\alpha = .92$). Perceived time pressure and subjective mental demand (perceived difficulty) were measured by an adapted and translated version of the NASA Task Load Index (NASA-TLX, Hart and Staveland, 1988) using respectively 1- and 3-item 5-point Likert scales.

For eye tracking, a Tobii computer monitor was used (Tobii 1750), accurate to 5 millimeters. In order to measure viewing behavior for both the interactive ad and the ongoing program, we defined two areas of interest (AOI) (see Figure 1).

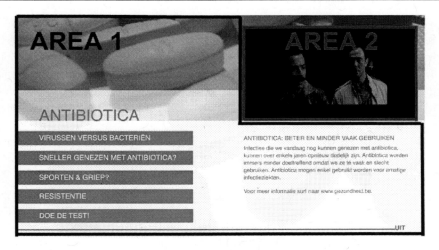

Figure 1. Screenshot of the simultaneous presentation of the Dedicated Advertising Location (DAL; defined as area 1) and the television program (defined as area 2).

This allowed us to register how much viewing attention was paid to each area in total (measured in seconds) and how many times the respondent's gaze jumped between the two areas.

RESULTS

Overall, respondents spent 96,5% of their total viewing time watching the interactive ad (area 1) and 3,5% watching the program (area 2). Time pressure resulted in a significantly lower total viewing time than no time pressure ($M_{\text{low time pressure}}$=172 seconds vs. $M_{\text{high time pressure}}$= 150 seconds, $t(67)$= 3.582, p= .001). Perceived time pressure was significantly different between the two time pressure conditions ($M_{\text{no time pressure}}$= 2.58 vs. $M_{\text{time pressure}}$= 3.48, $t(126)$= 4.320, $p<$ .001). In addition, time pressure had a significant influence on perceived difficulty of navigating in the DAL ($M_{\text{no time pressure}}$= 2.29 vs. $M_{\text{time pressure}}$= 2.54, $t(130)$= 2.176, p=.031).

The effect of program (in)congruence and time pressure and their interaction on ad viewing time was analyzed using ANOVA. The main effects of time pressure ($F(1, 113)$= 12.316, p=.001) and program congruence ($F(1, 113)$= 3.721, p=.056) on viewing time are significant. Subjects in the congruent condition spent significantly more time looking at the interactive ad than subjects in the incongruent condition ($F(1, 113)$= 3.721, p=.056;

M_congruent= 147sec vs. M_incongruent= 137sec), supporting H1a. There is also a significant main effect of time pressure ($F(1, 110)$= 12.504, p=.001) and program congruence ($F(1, 110)$= 5.501, p=.021) on gaze jumps. Viewers in the congruent condition jumps more frequently between the ad and the program than viewers of the incongruent condition (M_congruent=.132 jumps/sec vs. M_incongruent=.101 jumps/sec, $t(109)$=2.142, p=.034). This result supports H1b.

The assumption that the congruent program condition increases cognitive load and the time spent in the DAL was further supported by two additional analyses. Self-reported mental demand (perceived difficulty) (e.g. *'going through the interactive information was easy/difficult for me'*) was higher in the congruent (M= 2.7) than in the incongruent condition (M= 2.4), although this effect was not significant at conventional levels ($t(131)$= 1.621, p= .107). Perceived difficulty has been successfully used by past researchers to measure (cognitive) load (cf. Borg et al., 1971). Although the overall interaction effect in the ANOVA is not significant ($F(1, 113)$= 1.697, p=.195), post hoc tests show that in the incongruent condition, the level of time pressure has a smaller and insignificant effect on ad viewing time (M_low time pressure= 131 vs. M_high time pressure= 144, $t(54)$=1.578, p=.120) than in the congruent condition. In the latter, time pressure has a significant negative effect on ad viewing time (M_low time pressure= 162 vs. M_high time pressure= 135, $t(56)$=3.369, p=.001) (see Figure 2). This supports H2.

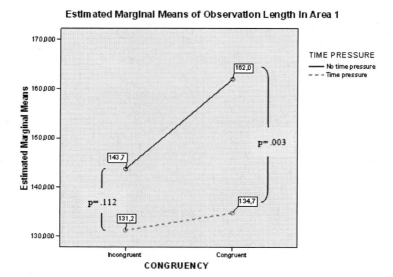

Figure 2. Interaction effect between congruence and time pressure on ad viewing time.

Finally, the incongruent condition leads to significantly higher involvement with the message than the congruent condition (M_congruent= 3.36 vs. M_incongruent= 3.58, $t(130)= 2.030$, $p=.044$), confirming H3a. Increasing time pressure leads to lower involvement, but this effect is not significant (M_low time pressure= 3.52 vs. M_high time pressure= 3.39, $t(130)=1.218$, $p= .225$). H3b is not supported.

CONCLUSION

This study shows that when viewers are simultaneously exposed to a thematically congruent program and an interactive advertisement, they devote more visual attention to the ad and jump more between the ad and the program than when the ad is processed in an incongruent context. Corroborating findings in this study support the idea that this is the result of interference effects and increased processing difficulty. When viewers want to process the ad information in a thematically congruent context, they are hindered and distracted by this program context that 'melts down' with the information in the ad, therefore needing more time to disentangle both. On the other hand, a thematically incongruent context is less interfering and distracting, and requires less time to process. These results are in line with the findings of Fitts et al. (1950), who predicted that gazes on a specific display element would be longer if the participant experienced difficulty extracting or interpreting information from that display element. The cognitive priming principle (Yi, 1990, 1993) suggests that congruence facilitates ad processing. In terms of viewing attention, that does not seem to be the case here. Further, we found that time pressure significantly reduces ad viewing time, more specifically when the ad and program context are congruent. Results show that, in general, time pressure increases cognitive load and perceived difficulty of processing the advertising information. When viewers have to process this information in a thematically congruent (and thus interfering) program context, this takes up even more cognitive capacity, resulting in substantially less ad viewing than when there is no time pressure. In an incongruent context, ad and program do not interfere, therefore demanding less cognitive capacity to deal with interference. As a result, the negative effect of time pressure on ad viewing time is much smaller. These results are confirmed by the fact that advertising involvement decreases in case of program congruence and under time pressure.

Our results show advertisers and media planners that in IDTV formats where ads and non-commercial content are shown simultaneously, it is advisable to thematically contrast the various components to which viewers are exposed. This will lead to less distraction, interference and cognitive load, enabling viewers to pay more attention to the commercial message. Furthermore, in these contrasting environments, ad viewing time diminishes less under time pressure than in congruent environments. So while traditional sequential congruent program-ad situations may benefit from cognitive priming effects, more novel simultaneous exposure formats, like IDTV, appear to be more effective in contrasting contexts. Thematically contrasting the various components to which viewers are exposed is not something that is often done in advertising, because marketers are afraid that by doing so, they will not reach the target group. However, this does not form a considerable threat in an IDTV context, where the advertisements during a commercial break are primarily aligned with the audience profile that corresponds to a certain television channel, rather than the content of the television program.

The limitations of the current study suggest directions for further research. For example, we only focused on viewing attention. Further research could investigate the relationship between this measured viewing time, self-reported attention and measures of recall of ad and program elements. In an unrestricted time situation, more viewing time may only be used to cope with interference, without any effect on recall. In a restricted time situation, this reduction of cognitive capacity may lead to lower recall. Cognitive load or more time needed to cope with interference may also lead to irritation. Therefore, the impact of viewing time on affective ad responses may be different, depending on what this time is used for (coping with incongruence or more in-depth processing of information). Finally, simultaneous exposure to various message formats like banners or streaming videos on one web page (as is often the case in reality), may also be used to study the effects of a set of similar or dissimilar ads on congruent or incongruent websites.

REFERENCES

Bellman, S., Varan, D. (2004). The impact of adding additional information to television advertising on elaboration, recall and persuasion. Paper presented at the ANZMAC Conference, Wellington.

Benson, L. III, Svenson, O. (1993). Post-decision consolidation following the debriefing of subjects about experimental manipulations affecting their prior decisions. *Psychological Research Bulletin*, 32, 1–13.

Bolls, P., Potter, R., Lang, A. (1996). Television arousal and memory: the effects of production pacing and arousing content on encoding, storage, and retrieval of television messages. In M. Gasser, Online proceedings of the 1996 Midwest Artificial Intelligence and Cognitive Science Conference.

Borg, G., Bratfisch, O., Dornic, S. (1971). On the problem of perceived psychology. *Scandinavian journal of psychology*, 12, 149-260.

Cauberghe, V., De Pelsmacker, P. (2008). The Impact of Banners on Digital Television: The Role of Program Interactivity and Product Involvement. *CyberPsychology*, 11 (1), 91-94.

Cauberghe, V., De Pelsmacker P., Janssens, W. (2009). *Simultaneous exposure to a program and advertising content in an interactive context: perceptual and semantic interference and reinforcement. Journal of Business Research*, article in press.

Chang, Y., Thorson, E. (2004). Television and web advertising synergies. *Journal of Advertising*, 33(2), 75-84.

Chowdhury, R., Finn, A., Olsen, D. G. (2007). Investigating the simultaneous presentation of advertising and television programming. *Journal of advertising*, 36 (3), 85-96.

Cox, D., Cox A. D. (2001). Communicating the consequences of early detection: the role of evidence and framing. *Journal of Marketing*, 65(July), 91–103.

Eysenck, M. W., Calvo, M. G. (1992). Anxiety and performance: The processing efficiency theory. *Cognition and Emotion*, 6, 409-434.

Fitts, P. M., Jones, R. E., Milton, J. L. (1950). Eye movements of aircraft pilots during instrument-landing approaches. *Aeronautical Engineering Review*, 9 (2), 24-29.

Furnham, A., Bergland, J., Gunter, B. (2002). Memory for television advertisements as a function of advertisement: programme congruity. *Applied Cognitive Psychology*, 16 (5), 525–45.

Gentry, L. (2007). Marketing and Eye-Tracking Machines: Research Opportunities for an Affordable Tool. *Journal of International Management Studies*, August, 60-65.

Hahn, M., Lawson, R., Lee, Y. G. (1992). The effects of time pressure and information load on decision quality. *Psychology and Marketing*, 9 (Sept/Oct), 365–378.

Hart, S. G., Staveland, L. (1988). Development of NASA-TLX (task load index): results of empirical and theoretical research, in: P. Hancock and N. Meshkati, Eds.: Human Mental Workload. Amsterdam, Netherlands: North-Holland Press, 239-250.

Herr, P. M. (1989). Priming price: prior knowledge and context effects. *Journal of Consumer Research*, 16 (June), 67–75.

Hornik, J. (1984). Subjective vs. objective times measures: A note on the perception of time in consumer behavior. *Journal of Consumer Research*, 11, 615-618.

Kumar, A. (2000). Interference effects of contextual cues in advertisements on memory for ad content. *Journal of Consumer Psychology*, 9 (3),155–66.

Lang, A. (2000). The limited capacity model of mediated message processing. *Journal of communication*, 50 (1), 46-70.

Lang, A., Newhagen, J., Reeves, B. (1996). Negative video as structure: emotion, attention, capacity, and memory. *Journal of Broadcasting and Electronic Media*, **40**, 460–477.

Lee, B. K., Lee, W. N. (2007). Decreasing advertising interference: the impact of comparable differences on consumer memory in competitive advertising environments. *Psychology and Marketing*, 24 (11), 919-945.

MacInnis, D., Moorman, C., Jaworski, B. (1991). Enhancing and measuring consumers' motivation, opportunity, and ability to process brand information from ads. *The Journal of Marketing*, 55 (4), 32-53.

Mandler, G. (1982). The structure of value: accounting for taste. In: Clark, MS., Fisk, ST., editors. Affect and cognition: the 17th annual Carnegie Symposium. Mahwah, NJ: Lawrence Erlbaum Associates, 1982, pp.203–230.

Maule, J. A., Svenson, O. (1993). Time Pressure and Stress in Human Judgment and Decision-Making. New York, United States: Plenum.

Ordonez, L., Lehman, B.III. (1997). Decisions under Time Pressure: how time constraint affects risky decision making. *Organizational Behavior and Human Decision Processes*,71 (August), 121–140.

Paas, F., van Merriënboer, J. J. G. (1994). Instructional control of cognitive load in the training of complex cognitive tasks. *Educational psychology review*, 6, 51-71.

Reading, N., Bellman, S., Varan, D., Winzar, H. (2006). Effectiveness of telescopic advertisements delivered by personal video recorders. *Journal of Advertising Research*, June, 217-227.

Sanbonmatsu, D. M., Fazio, R. H. (1991). Construct accessibility: determinants, consequences and implications for the media. In:

Responding to the screen: reception and reaction processes. Bryant J, Zillman D (eds). Erlbaum: Hillsdale, NJ; 45-62.

Schiessl, M., Duda, S., Tholke, A., Fischer, R. (2003). Eye tracking and its application in usability and media research, Sonderheft: Blickbewegung in MMI-interaktiv Journal, 6, 1-10.

Wegner, D. M., Erber, R., Zanakos, S. (1993). Ironic processes in the mental control of mood and moos-related thought. *Journal of personality and social psychology*, 65 (6), 1093.

Yi, Y. (1990). The effects of contextual priming in print advertisements. *Journal of Consumer Research*, 17 (2), 215-222.

Yi, Y. (1993). Contextual priming effects in print advertisements: The moderating role of prior knowledge. *Journal of Advertising*, 22 (l), 1-10.

In: Advertising
Editor: Evelyn P. Mann

ISBN 978-1-61324-679-5
© 2012 Nova Science Publishers, Inc.

Chapter 4

DIFFERENTIAL EFFECTS OF VISUAL AND VERBAL ELEMENTS IN ADVERTISEMENTS FOR NEW BRANDS AND EXTENSIONS

Nathalie Dens[1], Bianca Puttemans[1]
and Patrick De Pelsmacker[2]
[1]University of Antwerp, Belgium
[2]University of Antwerp and Ghent University, Belgium

ABSTRACT

The present study applies schema theory, the incongruity principle and the persuasion knowledge model to study consumer responses to visual and verbal elements in new products advertisements. Advertisements containing no, product related or (general) non-product related visuals, and no, basic or extended verbal information were tested for a line extension and a new brand.

The results show that brand strategy significantly moderates the effectiveness of verbal and visual elements in advertising. For new brands, non-product related visuals lead to the most negative responses.

For line extensions, the absence of visuals significantly reduces the attitude toward the ad. Consistent with enrichment, the added value of information is stronger for line extensions than for new brands. Implications and suggestions for further research are discussed.

INTRODUCTION

Innovation is a key success factor of a company's growth. Through new product introductions, companies try to satisfy customers and to obtain a significant competitive advantage. However, introducing new brands has major downsides. The total cost of introducing a new product is very high. In addition, a large amount of new product introductions still fail. By introducing extensions (new (versions of) products which make use of existing brand names), companies hope to leverage the reputation and awareness of the existing brand (parent brand) to the new product (line extension) (Aaker and Keller, 1990).

Advertising is a critical factor for any new product, including extensions (Kotler, 2000). Advertising may play a crucial role in determining whether the new product or line extension is successfully adopted by the target audience or not. Advertisements can be composed of different formats: they can contain both verbal information (text) and/or visual elements (pictures). In terms of verbal elements, the amount of information provided can vary greatly. In some advertisements, no information is provided on the particular product but the brand and perhaps model name. In others, basic information may be provided, such as the unique selling proposition. In still other advertisements, a large amount of information is provided on product features or benefits, to fully inform consumers on the product. This is often the case when the product is a search good or utilitarian product, and even more so if the product is new.

Visuals in advertising can be directly related to the advertised product, which means that there is a direct and clear link between the picture shown in the ad and the advertised product (as when a computer ad shows people using a computer). However, visuals in advertising can also be rather general and not particularly related to the advertised product. In this case, no clear product link can be found between the picture depicted in the ad and the advertised product (for example, when a computer ad shows people in a general or neutral context without any sign of a computer). Non-product related visuals are frequently used in transformational advertising, whose aim is to make products richer, warmer, more exciting, and/or more enjoyable, without necessarily focusing on the product or adding information (Puto and Wells, 1984). Non-product related advertising would normally also be considered rather incongruent with the advertised product. The use of mildly incongruent visuals is often applied in advertisements to attract attention and to stimulate information processing (Dens, De Pelsmacker, and Janssens, 2008; Mandler, 1982).

The effectiveness of different visual and verbal elements in advertising has been thoroughly researched (e.g., Brennan, 2008; Bulmer and Buchanan-Oliver, 2006). Most research, however, has focused on the positive and negative aspects of using ads that are either primarily visual or verbal in nature. In the current study, we aim to contribute to the literature by studying different combinations of visual and verbal advertising elements. In addition, we investigate the moderating role of brand strategy on the effectiveness of visual and verbal appeals (and their combinations) in terms of attitude toward the ad and advertising persuasiveness. In other words, the purpose of this study is to investigate which advertising formats in terms of the combination of the amount of verbal information and the nature of the visual used will result in a more positive attitude and higher persuasion for both new brands and line extensions.

THEORETICAL BACKGROUND AND HYPOTHESES

The Moderating Role of Brand Strategy on Consumer Responses to Advertising Visuals

Will using a product related visual, a non-product related visual, or no visual at all in advertisements for new products have a different impact in case of line extensions and new brands? Schema and categorization theories (Bartlett, 1932; Boush et al., 1987; Braun-LaTour and LaTour, 2004; Fiske and Pavelchak, 1986; Kent and Allen, 1994; Nan, 2006) can explain the processes that take place when people assess ads for line extensions and new brands with different types of visuals. According to categorization theory, people faced with an evaluative task will first attempt to classify the object within a certain category on the basis of salient cues (Fiske and Pavelchak, 1986; Park, Kim, and Kim, 2002; Rosch and Mervis, 1975). A brand name can serve as a category label and thus lead to a category-based evaluation of a new product, i.e. the extension (e.g., Maheswaran, Mackie, and Chaiken, 1992; Park et al., 2002). Category-based processing engenders a peripheral route to persuasion. In this case, the picture shown in an extension advertisement may serve as a peripheral cue (Miniard, Bhatla, Lord, Dickson, and Unnava, 1991). Most studies indeed find the effect of imagery in general on the evaluation of information to be positive (e.g., Babin and Burns, 1997). Under low advertising elaboration, affect-transfer is expected based on the presence of a visual or not, irrespective of the relevancy of the visual.

Following schema theory, a (brand) name represents a cognitive structure or schema, a network of associations built on organized knowledge about the brand (Braun-LaTour and LaTour, 2004). The use of visuals in advertising in general is consistent with brand schemas for most established brands. Stimuli which are congruent with the activated schema will result in more positive evaluations due to familiarity (Mandler, 1982; Meyers-Levy and Tybout, 1989). As such, even a non-product related visual stimulus may still be more effective than no visual for line extensions, as it is generally relatively more congruent with the brand schema, and visuals may be used as a peripheral cue (e.g., how-do-I-feel-about-it), which may engender positive effects. We hypothesize:

> H1a: In case of a line extension, an advertisement containing a congruent or incongruent visual results in a more positive attitude towards the ad (Aad) and a stronger persuasion (Apers) than an advertisement containing no visual.

How viewers interpret visual imagery in advertisements is contingent upon their knowledge resources (Bulmer and Buchanan-Oliver, 2006). For a new brand, by definition, no previous networks of associations or schemas to associate with exist, which will induce a different way of processing compared to extensions of existing brands (Campbell and Keller, 2003). For new, unfamiliar brands, categorization based on the brand name will be inhibited because of the absence of a brand category in consumers' minds. Categorization theory (Fiske and Pavelchak, 1986) then predicts that consumers will revert to more piecemeal processing of various features of the object (i.e. the new advertised product) as basis for forming an evaluation. As a result, new brands will engender more central and extensive processing, whereby consumers will evaluate the issue relevant arguments presented to them (Campbell and Keller, 2003; Dens and De Pelsmacker, 2010).

From this perspective, then, the visuals shown in ads for new brands serve as arguments, and the influence of their relevancy should grow as elaboration increases (Miniard et al., 1991). The persuasion knowledge model states that when consumers are relatively highly involved in processing a message, they are more likely to consider the appropriateness of the advertising strategy (Friestad and Wright, 1994). Under high elaboration, a non-product related visual may stimulate persuasion knowledge. If people try to actively process an advertisement for a new brand, the absence of the product in the visual stimulus may be perceived as manipulative. Especially for new brands, for which consumers have no existing schema, they might want to actually see product-relevant (visual) stimuli. Prior research has also noted that subjects have a tendency to make negative inferences when faced with missing information, especially when the presented information is perceived to be negatively correlated with the missing information (Bridges, Keller, and Sood, 2000). As they have no prior frame of reference, consumers will make inferences based mainly on the relevant cues provided in the advertisement (Kardes, Posavac, and Cronley, 2004). Therefore, the use of a visual which does not show the product may be inferred as the company is trying to hide something or distract them from the fact that it is not a good product. Consistent with the persuasion knowledge model, this will result in a negative evaluation (Friestad and Wright, 1994). Prior research has also argued that when viewers see advertising imagery that has no literal or obvious meaning, they refer back to their prior knowledge (Bulmer and Buchanan-Oliver, 2006). In the case of the new brands, prior knowledge is non-existent, which may cause frustration and lead to negative effect. We therefore predict:

> H1b. In case of a new brand, an advertisement containing an incongruent visual results in a more negative attitude towards the ad (Aad) and a weaker persuasion (Apers) than an advertisement containing a congruent or no visual.

ADDED VALUE OF VERBAL INFORMATION FOR LINE EXTENSIONS VERSUS NEW BRANDS

Based on categorization theory, if advertisements for new brands are indeed processed in a piecemeal or central fashion, verbal arguments or information should have a high impact on consumer evaluations. However, consumers' lack of an existing brand schema will inhibit the amount of information that can be processed about the brand and the advertisement. Campbell and Keller (2003) argue that individuals with prior knowledge structures or schemas are able and willing to encode new information on the same brand more easily than people confronted with the brand for the first time, as the former can link this new information to their existing framework of associations. Familiar brands typically have an elaborate and strong network of associations ('schema') in memory, which makes it easy for activation to spread. Therefore, people facing a familiar brand will more easily process new and extra information (Nabi, Roskos-Ewoldsen, and Carpentier-Dillman, 2008; Rucker and Petty, 2006; Wood and Kallgren, 1988). This is in line with the Enrichment Hypothesis (Johnson and Russo, 1984) that postulates that existing knowledge facilitates the learning of new information. Since, in the present study, the additional verbal information is positive and brand-supporting, we expect that this extra information will not only be absorbed more easily, but also lead to more positive evaluations. Individuals confronted with a novel issue cannot rely on existing nodes of knowledge in memory to be activated or existing knowledge to be enriched, which will obstruct the processing of new information. As people have a limited cognitive capacity (Lang, 2000), the fact that they still need to learn and encode information about the brand name itself, will cause that they have fewer resources available to process a lot of additional verbal information provided in the ad. We therefore expect:

> H2: The positive effect of extra verbal information on the attitude towards the ad (Aad) and ad persuasiveness (Apers) will be stronger for line extensions than for new brands

DESIGN AND PARTICIPANTS

A 2 (brand strategy: new brand or line extension) x 3 (visual format: no, non-product related or product related visual) x 3 (verbal information: no, basic or extended information) partial factorial between subjects design was conducted. Sixteen advertisements for a new laptop were developed (see Appendix for examples). The advertisements either showed a proposed new brand, Systemax, or a line extension of the existing brand Dell. The brands were chosen based on a pretest (n = 25) which showed that Dell was named by 64% of respondents in their top three of known computer brands, and that Systemax, a fictitious brand name, scored best in terms of appropriateness as a new brand name for computers out of three hypothetical brand names (M = 4.62). The brand name was accompanied by visual and/or verbal cues. The visuals were selected based on a separate pretest (n = 25), which showed that the relation of the picture to the product (5 items, e.g., the image is (not) consistent with a laptop, the image does (not) fit a laptop) was significantly higher for the product related visual (M = 5.54) than the nonrelated visual (M = 2.12) (t(24) = 10.133, p < .001). In addition, we chose stimuli showing the same models and tested that the visuals did not differ significantly in evoked positive feelings (warm, cozy, enthusiastic, energetic, positive feeling, t(24) = 1.074, p = .294) or negative feelings (sad, irritating, negative feeling, t(24) =

.041, p = .968), credibility (credible, skeptical (reversed), -, t(24)= .196, p= .846) and attitude toward the image as such (e.g., bad-good, don't like-like, negative-positive, t(24) = 1.316, p = .201) to avoid potential confounds. The nonrelated visual showed two people without the context of a computer, whereas the product related visual contained the same two people working at a computer. With regard to the verbal information format, the "basic information" condition consisted of a single text line stating the unique selling proposition of the new computer, whereas the "extended information" condition put forward a more detailed description of other product characteristics. The "no information" condition only showed the brand name and new model type. The information was given in Dutch as only Dutch-speaking Belgian respondents participated. A partial factorial design was set up as advertisements without any visual and without any information would have been meaningless. An online survey was conducted and a convenience sample of 542 Belgian respondents (53.7% women, aged 29.4 on average and 78.2% highly educated) were recruited. Respondents were randomly assigned to conditions. They were shown one of the 16 test ads and reported whether they knew the brand before, their attitude towards the ad (Aad) (bad-good, negative-positive, dislike-like; α = .95), the persuasiveness of the ad (Apers) (7 items adapted from Homer, e.g. (un)believable, (un)informative, (not) attention-grabbing, α = .85), and the manipulation check of visual congruency (for those having seen a visual) (A laptop is appropriate for what is shown in the picture, the picture used fits with a laptop, the picture is consistent with a laptop; α = .89) on seven-point semantic differential and Likert scales. Finally the respondents' gender, age and education were asked.

RESULTS

Manipulation Checks

In terms of brand familiarity, 97% of respondents indicated they were familiar with Dell, whereas 93% of respondents had never heard of Systemax (χ^2 = 432.94, p < .001). As in the pretest, the incongruent visual (M = 2.57) was also found to be less consistent with computers than the congruent visual (M = 4.12) (t(407) = 11.535, p < .001).

MAIN RESULTS

The results of the 2x3x3 MANOVA showed a marginally significant two-way interaction of Visual x Brand Strategy (F(2,541) = 2.64, p = .072, Figure 1) for the attitude towards the ad (Aad) and a significant two-way interaction of Visual x Brand Strategy for ad persuasiveness (Apers) (F(2,541) = 4.479, p = .012, Figure 2). Post hoc tests showed that, for a line extension, a product related visual led to a significantly more positive Aad (M = 4.23) than no visual (M = 3.80, p= .038). As expected, a non-product related visual scored moderately well (M = 4.02), and did not differ significantly from the other two conditions (p = .234). No significant differences in Apers of a line extension were found between the visual conditions (p = .291). Hypothesis 1a is confirmed for Aad, but not for Apers. For a new brand, a nonrelated visual resulted in a significantly more negative Aad (M = 3.59) than a product related visual (M = 4.02, p = .029), and was marginally more negative than no visual (M = 3.96, p = .094). The lowest Apers was found for a nonrelated visual (M = 3.62) when compared to a product related visual (M = 3.91, p = .072) and no visual (M = 4.45, (p < .001). Hypothesis 1b is confirmed.

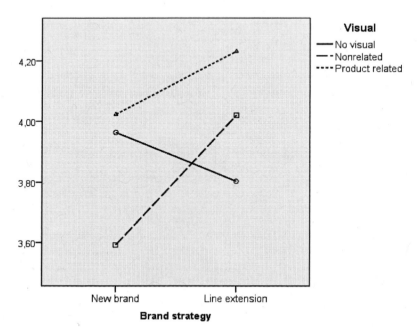

Figure 1. Visual x Brand Strategy interaction for the Attitude towards the ad (Aad).

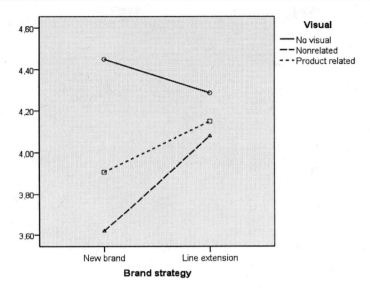

Figure 2. Visual x Brand Strategy interaction for Ad persuasiveness.

The MANOVA showed no significant Verbal information x Brand Strategy interaction ($F(2,541) = 1.44$, p = .238, Figure 3) for Aad, whereas a marginally significant effect ($F(2,541) = 2.863$, p= .058, Figure 4) was found for Apers. However, post hoc tests showed there were significant differences for both dependent variables. For a line extension, the "no verbal information" condition resulted in a more negative Aad (M = 3.66) than respectively the "basic information" condition (M = 4.17, p = .019) and the "extended information" condition (M = 4.18, p= .022). Furthermore, a lower Apers was found for the "no information" condition (M = 3.42) than for the "basic information" condition (M = 4.17, p< .001) and the "extended information" condition (M = 4.64, p < .001). The additional increase in Apers from basic to extended information was also significant for the line extension (p = .005). For a new brand, no significant differences in attitude towards the ad (Aad) were found between the different verbal information conditions. Although the highest Aad was indeed noted for an advertisement containing extended information (M = 3.98), followed by an ad containing basic information (M = 3.84, p = .483) and no information (M = 3.67, p = .129), none of the post hoc differences were significant. In terms of Apers, an advertisement containing no information (M= 3.42) scored significantly lower than an advertisement containing little information (M= 3.98) (p = .001) and an advertisement containing more information (M = 4.23) (p < .001). However, the additional increase in Apers from little to more information was not significant for new brands (p = .157). These results provide support for H2.

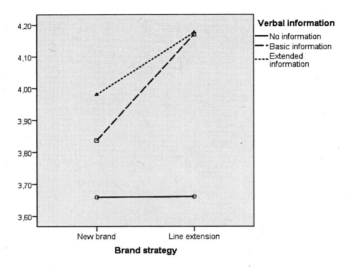

Figure 3. Verbal Information x Brand Strategy interaction for the Attitude towards the ad.

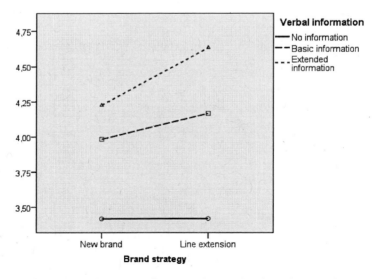

Figure 4. Verbal Information x Brand strategy interaction for Ad persuasiveness.

CONCLUSIONS AND SUGGESTIONS FOR FURTHER RESEARCH

Ads for a line extension using a product related or nonrelated visual lead to a more positive response than ads without a visual. This is consistent with schema theory (Braun-LaTour and LaTour, 2004) and the congruity principle (Mandler, 1982).

However, these effects were not found for ad persuasiveness. The extent to which an ad is persuasive is much more a cognitively-oriented response than the attitude towards the ad. Possibly, visuals are not instrumental for cognitive persuasion above and beyond the verbal arguments presented in the text. The results do show that the differences between visual stimuli in terms of persuasiveness are greater for new brands than for line extensions. This indicates that appropriate use of visual elements may be more important for new brands than of extensions.

As expected, for a new brand, incongruent visuals lead to a significant more negative Aad than ads with a congruent visual or no visual. This is in line with the Persuasion Knowledge mechanism (Friestad and Wright, 1994), as people are more highly motivated to process information about a new brand, an incongruent visual will more easily be seen as manipulative. Results on advertising evaluations of incongruity are conflicting (e.g., Janssens, De Pelsmacker, and Geuens, 2007; Lee and Sternthal, 1999). Our study shows that brand familiarity is an important moderator of the effect of incongruity on attitudes and persuasion. The results for Apers concerning a new brand are similar, however only marginally significant which can also be due to the fact that Apers is a cognitive measure.

In case of a line extension, an ad with extended verbal information resulted in a significantly stronger persuasiveness than an ad with basic or no information. For a new brand, the effect of adding verbal information is less pronounced. Interestingly, providing a little information in ads for new brands is as persuasive as providing a lot of information. This is a result that is markedly distinct from the line extension finding, and is consistent with the Enrichment Hypothesis (Johnson and Russo, 1984). People confronted with an advertisement for a new brand cannot rely on existing schemas in memory, which will obstruct the processing of too much new information, while existing knowledge about the brand facilitates the learning of even a lot of new information, which, if positive, leads to stronger persuasion. The results have implications for the advertising strategy of new brands and line extensions.

When advertising a line extension, congruent or mildly incongruent visuals should be combined with a lot of information. In new brand campaigns, providing too much information and especially incongruent visuals should be avoided. It should be noted that the current study only takes into account effects on advertising measures, Aad and persuasion. Although advertising responses are often believed to affect brand attitude and purchase intention, further research should look into the effects on product related measures and behavior. Further research is also needed to expand the current results and test the effects on memory, elaboration and cognition. This study focused on a product category that for most people qualifies as utilitarian and involving. Future research should investigate to what extent visuals and verbal information lead to other effects for different types of products, such as low involvement and hedonic product types. The visual stimuli used in the present study were relatively congruent in that they were not confusing or irrelevant. However, strongly incongruent ads or pictures are often used to attract the attention. Future studies could investigate how these attention-getting techniques have a different effect on the evaluative responses to new and existing brands.

APPENDIX: STIMULUS EXAMPLES

(a) Line extension, no visual, basic information

(b) New brand, nonrelated visual, no information

(c) Line extension, product related visual, extended information

REFERENCES

Aaker, D. A., and Keller, K. L. (1990). Consumer Evaluations of Brand Extensions. *Journal of Marketing, 54*(1), 27-41.

Babin, L. A., and Burns, A. C. (1997). Effects of print ad pictures and cpoy containing instructions to imagine on mental imagery that mediates attitudes. *Journal of Advertising, 16*(3), 33-44.

Bartlett, F. C. (1932). *Remembering: a study in experimental and social psychology*. New York, NY: Cambridge University Press.

Bishop, M., and Peterson, M. (2010). The Impact of Medium Context on Bilingual Consumers' Responses to Code-Switched Advertising. *Journal of Advertising, forthcoming*.

Boush, D. M., Shipp, S., Loken, B., Gencturk, E., Crockett, S., and Kennedy, E. (1987). Affect and generalization to similar and dissimilar brand extensions. *Psychology and Marketing, 4*(3), 225-237.

Braun-LaTour, K. A., and LaTour, M. S. (2004). Assessing the long-term impact of a consistent advertising campaign on consumer memory. *Journal of Advertising, 33*(2), 49-61.

Brennan, I. (2008). Brand placement in novels. *International Journal of Advertising, 27*(4), 495-509.

Bridges, S., Keller, K. L., and Sood, S. (2000). Communication strategies for brand extensions: Enhancing perceived fit by establishing explanatory links. *Journal of Advertising, 29*(4), 1-11.

Bulmer, S., and Buchanan-Oliver, M. (2006). Advertising across Cultures: Interpretations of Visually Complex Advertising. *Journal of Current Issues and Research in Advertising, 28*(1), 57-71.

Campbell, M. C., and Keller, K. L. (2003). Brand familiarity and advertising repetition effects. *Journal of Consumer Research, 30*(2), 292-301.

Dens, N., and De Pelsmacker, P. (2010). How advertising strategy affects brand and USP recall for new brands and extensions. *International Journal of Advertising, 29*(2), 165-194.

Dens, N., De Pelsmacker, P., and Janssens, W. (2008). Exploring consumer reactions to incongruent mild disgust appeals. *Journal of Marketing Communications, 14*(4), 249-269.

Fiske, S. T., and Pavelchak, M. A. (1986). Category-based versus piecemeal-based affective responses: Developments in schema-triggered affect. In R. M. Sorrentino and E. T. Higgins (Eds.), *The handbook of motivation and cognition, Volume 1: Foundations of social behavior* (pp. 167-203). New York: Guilford.

Friestad, M., and Wright, P. (1994). The persuasion knowledge model: How people cope with persuasion attempts. *Journal of Consumer Research, 21*, 1-31.

Jaffe, L. J., Jamieson, L. F., and Berger, P. D. (1992). Impact of Comprehension, Positioning, and Segmentation on Advertising Response. *Journal of Advertising Research, 32*(3), 24-33.

Janssens, W., De Pelsmacker, P., and Geuens, M. (2007). *Does a Medium Context Have a Priming or an Interference Effect? It Depends on How You Look At It.* Paper presented at the Advances in Consumer Research, North America.

Johnson, E. J., and Russo, E. J. (1984). Product familiarity and learning new information. *Journal of Consumer Research, 11*(June), 542-550.

Kardes, F. R., Posavac, S. S., and Cronley, M. L. (2004). Consumer inference: A review of processes, bases, and judgment contexts. *Journal of Consumer Psychology, 14*(3), 230-256.

Kent, R. J., and Allen, C. T. (1994). Competitive interference effects in consumer memory for advertising: the role of brand familiarity. *Journal of Marketing, 58*(3), 97-105.

Kotler, P. (2000). *Marketing management*: Upper Saddle River, NJ: Prentice-Hall.

Lang, A. (2000). The limited capacity model of mediated message processing. *Journal of Communication, 50*(1), 46-70.

Lee, A. Y., and Labroo, A. A. (2004). The Effect of Conceptual and Perceptual Fluency on Brand Evaluation. *Journal of Marketing Research, 41*(2), 151-165.

Lee, A. Y., and Sternthal, B. (1999). The effects of positive mood on memory. *Journal of Consumer Research, 26*(2), 115-127.

MacInnis, D. J., and Jaworski, B. J. (1989). Information processing from advertisements: Toward an integrative framework. *Journal of Marketing, 53*(4), 1-23.

Maheswaran, D., Mackie, D. M., and Chaiken, S. (1992). Brand name as a heuristic cue: The effects of task importance and expectancy confirmation on consumer judgments. *Journal of Consumer Psychology, 1*(4), 317-336.

Mandler, G. (Ed.). (1982). *The structure of value: accounting for taste.* Hillsdale, NJ: Erlbaum.

Meyers-Levy, J., and Tybout, A. M. (1989). Schema congruity as a basis for product evaluation. *Journal of Consumer Research, 16*(1), 39-54.

Miniard, P. W., Bhatla, S., Lord, K. R., Dickson, P. R., and Unnava, H. R. (1991). Picture-based persuasion processes and the moderating role of involvement. *Journal of Consumer Research, 18*(June), 92-107.

Nabi, R. L., Roskos-Ewoldsen, D., and Carpentier-Dillman, F. (2008). Subjective knowledge and fear appeal effectiveness: implications for message design. *Health Communication, 23*(2), 191-201.

Nan, X. L. (2006). Success factors of line extensions and fast- moving consumer goods. *European Journal of Marketing, 33*(5/6), 450-469.

Paivio, A., Clark, J. M., and Lambert, W. E. (1988). Bilingual dual- coding theory and semantic repetition effects on recall. *Journal of Experimental Psychology: Learning memory and cognition, 14*, 163-172.

Park, J.-W., Kim, K.-H., and Kim, J. (2002). Acceptance of brand extensions: Interactive influences of product category similarity, typicality of claimed benefits, and brand relationship quality. *Advances in Consumer Research, 29*(1), 190-198.

Puto, C. P., and Wells, W. D. (1984). Informational and Transformational Advertising: The Differential Effects of Time. *Advances in Consumer Research, 11*(1), 638-643.

Rosch, E., and Mervis, C. B. (1975). Family resemblances: Studies in the internal structure of categories. *Cognitive Psychology, 7*, 573-605.

Rucker, D. D., and Petty, R. E. (2006). Increasing the effectiveness of communications to consumers: Recommendations based on elaboration likelihood and attitude certainty perspectives. *Journal of Public Policy and Marketing, 25*(1), 39-52.

Wood, W., and Kallgren, C. A. (1988). Communicator attributes and persuasion: Recipients' access to attitude- relevant information in memory. *Personality and Social Psychology Bulletin, 14*(1), 172-182.

In: Advertising
Editor: Evelyn P. Mann
ISBN 978-1-61324-679-5
© 2012 Nova Science Publishers, Inc.

Chapter 5

BRIDGING THE GAP BETWEEN DREAM AND REALITY: STAKES AND ADVERTISING STRATEGIES

Virgine Villeneuve Anaudin
Franco-Australian Centre for International Research in Marketing
FACIREM EA 1707, Réunion Island University, France

ABSTRACT

Many consumers do not buy what they dream about. Thus, to attract the consumer without creating disappointment, we need to reconcile dream and reality.

However, the compromise between dream and reality is difficult to achieve because it can differ significantly according to individuals, culture and countries. The definition of an efficient global strategy therefore leads us to examine these differences. In this study, advertising discourse is used as a means to reconcile the gap between the bought and the dream product. Means-end chains make it possible to determine the buying and the dream processes.

A clustering analysis method, MPC method (Aurifeille, 2004), was used to determine reconcilable processes. Results suggest that narcissistic people are an ideal target for global marketing strategies since they do not feel a gap: one single advertising discourse corresponds to both the bought and the dream product.

Among individuals who have a significant gap, only less narcissistic and older people can bear a wide gap. The structure of the discourse which reconciles both the bought and the dream product is examined.

Keywords: Advertising discourse, means-end chains, clustering, personality.

1. INTRODUCTION

The needs that motivate a purchase include both reality and dream. Indeed, a need is sparked off by a feeling of something lacking and the best way to satisfy this need is to buy the dream product (Kotler et al., 1997). For instance, an individual needs a car to go to work: he can buy an ordinary car only for its initial features. As he wants to be perceived as a rising young executive, he would rather have a special car (4WD). Thus, to attract the consumer without creating disappointment, one needs to reconcile dream and reality. More than simply filling a gap, the product must be a personalised response to the need. It is a real challenge because there is a gap between what consumers do (reality) and what they would like to do (dream).

The frustration developed by this gap can be prejudicial to firms: firms whose product remains a dream, as well as those whose product is bought. In the first case, the product becomes a dream object but is not bought, while in the second case, it is bought but does not bring entire satisfaction.

How to reconcile dream and reality so that the gap between the bought and the dream product remains bearable?

Compromise between dream and reality is difficult to achieve because it can differ significantly according to individuals. Indeed, needs are limited, but the way to satisfy them varies hugely from culture to culture (Kotler et al., 1997). Thus, the dream product is different depending on the country.

The definition of an efficient global strategy therefore leads us to examine these differences, since knowing the processes which link values to behaviour can help to delimit markets (Vinson, et al., 1977; Aurifeille et al., 1998). Thus, in order to be able to act, we need to apply a single, simple and explanatory model to all kinds of behaviour (Aurifeille, 1997). Consequently, we must specify the consumer's behaviour in respect of the dream-reality dilemma, so as to identify homogeneous consumer behaviour segments and to adapt global marketing accordingly.

Advertising is a fundamental element of marketing because it persuades consumers (to buy) through communicating self-relevant messages (Reynolds et al., 1995). So, it can be a way of reaching a compromise between the dream and the bought product as it makes it possible to create and to manage the image of the product (Reynolds et al., 1984a). It can be a moderator when it contributes to making the gap between dream and reality bearable. But it can also make the situation worse when it attributes disproportionate and false qualities to a product.

The quality of the advertising message depends on language components and the way they are assembled (Percy, 1988). Therefore, advertising must propose a message based on consumer expectation in order to solve the dream-reality dilemma.

Means-end chains connect product attributes to consumer values (Gutman, 1982). They provide a link between perception and emotion, thus making it possible to determine the consumer decision-making process (Reynolds et al., 1984b). Also, knowing the means-end chains of a consumer group puts a certain message at our disposal (elements and sequences) (Aurifeille, 1997). By formulating his means-end chain, the consumer elaborates his own logic. So, by basing the advertising message on such logic, one can expect less resistance from the consumer (Aurifeille et al., 1998). If the advertising message is based on the means-end chain reconciling the consumer's perception of the bought product and the one of his dreams, we can expect to reduce consumer frustration. Indeed, the advertising message praises a product which bridges the gap between dream and reality.

2. MEANS END-CHAÏNS: A TOOL FOR ANALYSING THE CONSUMER MESSAGE: THE MEANS-END CHAIN MODEL AND METHOD OF ANALYSIS

2.1. The Means-End Chain Model

Consumers choose products that are the means to achieve a desired state (Gutman, 1982). The means-end chain model makes it possible to define this decision-making process (Reynolds, et al., 1984b) by connecting values (end) to product attributes (means) (Reynolds et al., 1988).

A means-end chain is defined as the connection between product attributes, consequences for the consumer and personal values. Attributes are features or aspects of products or services (Reynolds et al., 1984c). Consequences arise out of people consuming products or services (Gutman, 1984). Values are "enduring beliefs that a specific mode of conduct or end-state of existence is personally or socially preferable to an opposite or converse mode of conduct or end-state of existence" (Rokeach, 1973).

Olson et al. (1983) distinguish abstract and concrete attributes, functional and psychosocial consequences and finally instrumental and terminal values.

All of these links are not present in every case (Olson et al., 1983) (see Figure 1).

This poses several problems (Aurifeille, 2004): to avoid sparse data bases (containing mainly zero values), researchers have proposed a variety of means-end data collecting techniques that constrain the format of the replies (number and content of steps). However, this kind of approach may impede the emergence of shorter processes. This also poses the problem of assigning items to a priori steps. Thus, it is necessary to avoid arbitrary constraints. A means-end chain comprises at least one beginning item and one terminal item (Aurifeille, 2004).

Means-end chains are identified through the laddering method (Reynolds et al., 1988). This involves a technique of in-depth interviewing to determine the links between attributes, consequences and values by repeating the same question *"Why is this important to you?"*.

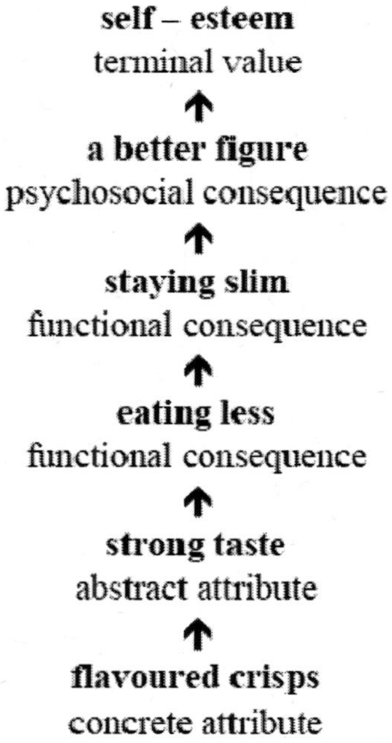

self – esteem
terminal value
↑
a better figure
psychosocial consequence
↑
staying slim
functional consequence
↑
eating less
functional consequence
↑
strong taste
abstract attribute
↑
flavoured crisps
concrete attribute

Figure 1. Example of a means-end chain (Reynolds et al., 1988).

Laddering is one of the most useful qualitative methods for advertising communication since it provides an opportunity for consumers to respond to choice situations in their own words and express their own feelings (Gengler et al., 1995). Thus, reproduction of the means-end chain can improve advertising persuasion (Young et al., 1975). Consumers perceive the personal relevance and desirability of product attributes in terms of their association with the personal consequences of product use. Similarly, the relevance and desirability of personal consequences are derived from their association with a consumer's personal values. Thus, the strength of the association of the means-end information communicated and an advertisement will contribute to explaining the persuasive power of a brand (Reynolds et al., 1995).

From an empirical point of view, using means-end chains makes it possible to determine the chain of the bought brand (reality) and that of the preferred brand (dream). Thus, we have an advertising message based exactly on the product bought and another one based on the dream product. Thanks to the association between these two processes, it is possible to examine the gap between dream and reality. The choice of analysis method will help determine the possible reconciliation between the buying process and the dream process.

2.2. The Method of Analysis

To determine the gap between the buying process and the dream process, we need to measure the distance which separates them, in order to make groups. If both buying and dream processes are in the same group, there is no gap, whereas if they are in different groups there is a significant gap. Clustering is an appropriate means since it categorises the population in a way which maximises the homogeneity of consumer profiles within groups, while at the same time maximising the heterogeneity of consumer profiles between groups (Aurifeille, 2000). However, in the case of the means-end chain, it is all uphill work (Aurifeille, 1994).

Indeed, for mean-end chains, it is a question of determining groups of processes and not of basic data. Furthermore, each individual is characterised by several processes, the length of which may vary (Aurifeille, 1997).

The MPC method (Means-end Process Clustering) (Aurifeille, 2004) is an appropriate approach since it takes into account the processes and requires no arbitrary constraints applied to steps and content. The clustering of means-end chains is carried out by considering their vectors of input-output probability. Then, the means-end chain prototype is determined in each cluster as being the one that represents as closely as possible any chain belonging to the cluster. Therefore, a centroid-based criterion is used to estimate internal validity: the ratio of the average within-cluster distance by the average between-cluster distance.

The possible prototypes are means-end chains, which offer the opportunity to find an advertising message reconciling dream and reality. Indeed, if both the buying and the dream processes are in the same cluster, the prototype represents these two processes.

On the contrary, if there is a significant gap between the dream and the buying process because they are in different clusters and two different prototypes correspond to each of them, MPC enables us to reach a compromise using constraint clustering. In this approach, the cluster barycentres in which individuals are classified are limited in number and fixed in advance. Thus we can carry out a cluster analysis on the individuals whose processes are in two different groups and constrain the cluster barycentres. The authorised centres are, for instance, the dream processes only. Thus we can determine whether there is a possible compromise available for some individuals. Indeed, individuals whose processes are in the same cluster can bear a gap between the buying and the dream messages, since there is a process which corresponds to each of them. Nevertheless, individuals whose processes are always in two different clusters cannot bear a significant gap between the buying and the dream messages.

3. ANALYSIS AND RESULTS

3.1. Analysis

This analysis aims to carry out an initial clustering (hereafter "primary clustering") of the entire sample (bought product chain and dream product chain) and thereafter only take an interest, in individuals whose chains (bought product chain and dream product chain) are not in the same cluster. Indeed, these individuals have such a gap between the product they buy and the one they dream about that their two chains are in different clusters and consequently a different advertising message is appropriate to each of them. In this case, no message can reconcile dream and reality.

To produce an advertising message that presents a tolerable gap between dream and reality, we proceed to a second clustering (hereafter "secondary clustering") on this subset. This is a constraint clustering which only accepts as prototype chains (barycentres) the dream processes of these individuals. Indeed, we suppose that to be attractive, advertising needs to make people dream. Thus, the advertising message cannot be based on the bought brand.

Two cases are possible:

- Individuals for whom the two processes always correspond to two different means-end discourses. No message can reconcile the means-end chains of their bought and dream product.
- Individuals for whom the two processes (the bought and the dream product) correspond to the same means-end discourse. The prototype chain of the cluster to which they belong represents the message that reconciles both the bought and the dream processes.

3.2. Data Collection

If consumption of a product is conspicuous in public and is socially visible, consumers are likely to use the visibility of the product to symbolically communicate something about themselves to others (Lee, 1990). They will therefore be more attentive to the information and to the choice of the product. An automobile owner's perception of his car is essentially congruent with his perception of himself (Birdwell, 1968). In choosing his automobile, the consumer expresses something that concerns him. Thus, the car seems to be a product well-adapted to the study. Furthermore, the car industry is the second biggest advertiser in the French market.

Data collection was carried out through means-end interviews. A preliminary study was carried out on twenty individuals so as to determine product items (attributes, consequences and values). In-depth interviews made it possible to focus on 51 items (see Appendix 1). Models of cars were selected according to their share of the national market. Thus, the 15 most frequently sold brands were retained.

104 individuals were interviewed through the means-end chain procedure using QCMF software (FACIREM, 2003). This procedure consists of suppressing all step-related constraint by proposing all the items at each stage of the chain. The respondent chooses an item and the same list is proposed at the next question. The chain ends as soon as a terminal value is reached (Manin et al., 2003). Two chains were collected for each respondent: one for the bought car and one for the dream car, making a total number of 208 chains.

4. RESULTS

4.1. Primary Clustering (Entire Sample)

For the primary clustering, the 5-cluster solution indicators are satisfactory (see Table 1). The correlation and the adjustment are high; the convergence rate reaches 95%.

For more than half of the sample (65 individuals), the chain of the bought product and the chain of the dream product are situated in two different clusters. This confirms the observation that individuals do not always buy what they dream about.

4.2. Secondary Clustering (Subset of 65 Individuals)

For secondary clustering results, we chose the 3-cluster solution. Not only are the indicators acceptable (see Table 2), but for more than half of the sample (35 individuals), the two processes are situated in the same cluster. This result confirms the hypothesis that an advertising message can reconcile both the bought product and the dream product.

This first empirical test confirms that, for the entire sample, more than half of the individuals experience such a gap between the bought and the dream product that a different means-end message corresponds to each of them. We can see therefore that these individuals cannot bear a significant gap.

Nevertheless, the size of the bearable gap differs according to individuals. Indeed, more than half of this segment tolerates a more important gap. For 35 individuals out of 65, one means-end discourse reconciles both the bought and the dream product message.

Thus, these individuals have reconcilable processes, since one can reduce their frustration by adapting the advertising discourse. There exists a message which does not exactly correspond to either the buying or the dream process, but which combines both.

To develop managerial involvement, we need to identify these individuals: what kind of person are they? How to recognise them?

We also need to know what kind of advertising is appropriate for them? Is it a short or a long means-end process? Is it an abstract or a concrete process?

Table 1. Choice criteria for primary clustering

Choice criteria	Primary clustering (104 individuals) 5 clusters
K-biserial	
(1 – average within / average between cluster)	0.65391
Adjustment	0.90415
(1- within / between cluster)	
Convergence rate	95.72
Number of individuals	
Whose chains correspond to two means-end processes	65

Table 2. Choice criteria for secondary clustering

Choice criteria	Secondary clustering (65 individuals) 3 clusters
K-biserial	
(1 – average within / average between clusters)	0.64287
Adjustment	
(1- within / between cluster)	0.82416
Convergence rate	90.20
Number of individuals	
Whose chains correspond to the same means-end process	35

5. STRATEGICAL ISSUES: IDENTIFICATION OF CONSUMERS WITH RECONCILABLE PROCESSES

5.1. Brand Personality

Self relevance and desirability of brand information is presumed to be the basis for consumer preference and choice (Gutman, 1982). Thus, advertising strategies attempt to create self-relevant messages. Advertising tends to associate personality dimensions with brands (Plummer, 1984) because certain brands and individual personality traits are similar (Ferrandi et al., 2002). This increases the personal relevance of a brand for the consumer (Levy, 1959).

Figure 2. Example of an advertisement using personality traits.

Furthermore, advertising messages that are congruent with an individual's self-concept are more effective than incongruent ones (Hong et al., 1995; Wang et al., 1997). Aaker (1997) defines brand personality as "the set of human characteristics associated with a brand". For instance, the advertisement below shows a black car parked in the countryside, near a meadow. In the background, we can see a herd of white cars. One can easily imagine the herd of sheep and the wolf. This car symbolises strength, ferociousness and the aggressiveness of the owner, whereas the white cars symbolise a herd of weak individuals, ordinary people who have no social recognition. Consequently, the consumer may identify himself with the brand. However, depending on their personality, different people evaluate products displayed in advertisements differently (Mizerski et al., 1979). Thus, from a theoretical point of view, personality can help to differentiate people. Individuals who can bear a gap between the bought and the dream product may have a different personality from those who cannot bear a gap or those who do not experience a gap.

5.2. Consumer Personality

Most behaviour is connected to tension inside the personality system. The personality is composed of three elements, which work together to produce all complex behaviour (Freud, 1993):

Id
Superego
Ego

The Id constitutes the irrational and emotional part of the mind, the Superego stores and enforces rules and the Ego is an intermediate authority. The ego implements strategies of defence in order to maintain the consistency and functioning of the individual. The way in which the Ego compromises and negotiates between the Id and the Superego explains the great variety of consumer behaviour (Kassarjian, 1971).

Conflicts between the Id and the Superego reflect the opposition between the external world and the psychic world (Freud, 1993). This turmoil creates anxiety and frustration which the Ego has to cope with by elaborating defence strategies. To overcome basic anxiety and frustration, people develop defence strategies, each of which involves a constellation of behaviour patterns, personality traits, sets of belief about human nature and human values (Horney, 1945). Narcissism, compliance and aggressiveness are three defence strategies also used in advertising alongside brand personality.

5.3. Narcissism

Narcissistic people seek to master life by self admiration and through the exercise of charm. They have an unquestioned belief in their abilities and feel that there is no one that they cannot win over. Their insecurity is manifested in the fact that they may speak incessantly of their exploits or wonderful qualities and need endless confirmation of their self-esteem in the form of admiration and devotion. Their bargain is that if they hold onto their dreams and their exaggerated claims for themselves, life is bound to give them what they want. They admire themselves in the mirror that their surroundings represent for them. These individuals tend to escape into fantasy and mythomania.

As a result, this kind of individual may not experience a gap between the bought and the dream product since he or she lives in fantasy. Thus, what they buy is obviously what they dream about.

5.4. Compliance

People in whom compliant trends are dominant try to overcome their basic anxiety by gaining affection and approval and controlling others through their dependency. Their values are those of kindness, sympathy, love, generosity, unselfishness, humility; while egotism, ambition, callousness, unscrupulousness, wielding of power are abhorred. This type of individual seeks the affection and the approval of others.

As compliant people want to be accepted and approved of by others, one can expect them to consume the same way as other group members so as not to be rejected. Their dream product is the product bought by the group they wish to integrate. One can therefore expect that they cannot tolerate a gap between the bought and the dream product.

5.5. Aggressiveness

Individuals that practice the strategy of aggressiveness are motivated chiefly by a need for vindictive triumphs. They feel that the world is an arena, where only the fittest survive and the strong annihilate the weak. They are competitive, ruthless and cynical. They do not count on the world to give them anything.

As their aim is to succeed, they are ready to accept a compromise so as to win. One can expect aggressive people to be able to bear a gap between the bought and the dream product.

5.6. Analysis

To identify narcissistic, compliant or aggressive individuals, we need to know the defence strategy they use. Given that each strategy is characterised by character traits, modes of behaviour and values, we can choose to use individual values to represent the different types of individual. Values are appropriate to the study of behaviour because they are conscious and admissible (Aurifeille et al., 1998), and enduring (Rokeach, 1973). Therefore, they are the substitute for motivation (Howard, 1994). Furthermore, they have been determined thanks to the means-end chains collection.

A questionnaire on values was handed out. The 20 values, retained for the means-end collection, were noted 3 times on a semantic bipolar scale of 7 modes. These values were noted according to the strategy used by consumers: narcissism, compliance or aggressiveness. According to the way the question is formulated, one can find the three styles of defence[1].

---

[1] Being independent is one of the values which determines my existence -
- not at all /-/-/-/-/-/-/-/ totally

5.7. Results

In the primary clustering, individuals whose two chains are in the same cluster are more narcissistic (average score 101) than others (average score of 97) ($p = 0.03$). These individuals do experience a gap between the bought and the dream product.

In the secondary clustering, we notice that individuals whose two chains are in the same cluster and who tolerate a more significant gap than others are less narcissistic (average score of 95 against an average score of 100 for others, $p = 0.05$). We also notice that they are older (8 years more on average, $p = 0.000$).

Among the individuals who, in the primary typology, have their two chains in two clusters, are less narcissistic people will be more apt to receive an advertising message presenting a relatively significant gap between the bought and the dream product. Therefore, one can reach a compromise for less narcissistic people.

6. IDENTIFICATION OF THE PROCESS WHICH RECONCILES THE DREAM AND THE BOUGHT PRODUCT

For instance, for individual No. 1 (example drawn from the results): in the primary clustering, an advertising message corresponds to his buying process and another corresponds to his dream process.

The advertising message of his buying process is:

Size → Easy Handling → Avoiding Breakdowns → Saving money → Fulfilling Oneself

The advertising message of his dream process is:

Solidity / Sturdiness → Security

Others consider that being independent is one of the values which determines my existence -
- not at all /-/-/-/-/-/-/-/ totally
I'd like others to consider that being independent is one of the values which determines my existence -
- not at all /-/-/-/-/-/-/-/ totally

This individual feels such a gap between the dream and the bought product that a different message corresponds to each of them. Nevertheless, this individual is less narcissistic than the average, as well as older. He therefore tolerates a relatively significant gap between the dream and the bought product.

The message that reconciles the dream and the buying processes is:

Solidity / Sturdiness → Saving money →Security

In this example, we notice that the three chains have different morphologies. The advertising speech of the bought product is long and functional (1 concrete attribute, 3 functional consequences and 1 terminal value), the one of the dream product is short (2 items), while the one that conciliates the two is balanced (3 items: 1 concrete attribute, 1 functional consequence, 1 terminal value). These observations can be generalised to the totality of the subset (see Table 3).

Prototype chains of the bought product are longer and more functional. They have a high number of levels. Functional consequences occupy a preponderant place, however they have no abstract attributes and nearly no instrumental values.

The prototype chains of the dream product are shorter. Although they have more functional items than abstract ones, these chains are relatively well-balanced. They contain no abstract attribute and virtually no functional consequences or instrumental values.

The prototype chains that reconcile the bought and the dream product are of average length. They comprise more abstract attributes than the bought and the dream prototypes. However, they have more functional attributes. The number of levels is similar to the bought prototype. No instrumental values are included in these chains.

Thus, in order to make an effective advertising campaign that will reduce consumer frustration, advertisers have to target less narcissistic individuals. The advertising message must contain 3 steps and stress the concrete benefits that using the product may bring to the consumer.

Table 3. ANOVA of the processes of less narcissistic people

Means (Intervals of confidence)	Bought prototypes	Dream prototypes	Prototypes that reconcile both bought and dream processes	p
No. of items	4.5 (4.2 – 4.8)	2.3 (2 – 2.6)	3 (3 – 3)	0.000
No. of abstract items	1 (1 – 1)	1.05 (1 – 1.1)	1.1 (1- 1.2)	0.055
No. of functional items	3.5 (3.2 – 3.8)	1.3 (1 – 1.6)	1.8 (1.7 –2)	0.000
No. of steps	3 (3 – 3)	2.2 (2 – 2.3)	3 (3 – 3)	0.000
No. of abstract attributes	0 (0 – 0)	0 (0 – 0)	0.14 (0 – 0.2)	0.005
No. of functional consequences	2.3 (1.9 – 2.7)	0.3 (0 – 0.6)	0.9 (0.7 – 1)	0.000
No. of instrumental values	0.2 (0 – 0.3)	0.03 (-0.03 – 0.09)	0 (0 – 0)	0.003

7. DISCUSSION

Narcissism appears as the defence strategy that has the greatest effect on the bearable gap between the bought and the dream product. As far as the most narcissistic individuals are concerned, the same advertising message corresponds to both the bought and the dream product. These individuals do not experience a gap between dream and reality because they confuse dream and reality. As they live in fantasy, the product they buy is their dream product.

Among individuals who feel a significant gap between the bought and the dream product, only less narcissistic have reconcilable processes. The advertising message which reconciles both their bought and their dream product is balanced.

However, it will contain more abstract items than the bought message and the dream message. This message contains functional consequences, but no instrumental values.

CONCLUSION

In this study, the advertising message is used as a means to reconcile the gap between the dream product and the bought product. Means-end chains made it possible to determine the bought and the dream processes, whereas the analysis method MPC was used to find reconcilable processes.

Results show that individuals who do not feel a gap between dream and reality are more narcissistic than the average. Thus, these individuals represent an ideal target since only one advertising message corresponds to what they buy and to what they dream about.

However, more than half of individuals perceive a significant gap between bought and dream products, since their advertising messages are different. However, it is clear that among these individuals, the less narcissistic ones tolerate a relatively important gap between the bought and the dream product. Indeed, there is an advertising message that does not correspond either to their bought product, or to their dream product, but which is close to both. This message contains as many items as steps (3), it emphasises the benefits linked to using the product, whereas individual qualities are not mentioned.

Concerning global marketing, the managerial consequences are obvious: firms have to first target narcissistic individuals, since they represent an ideal target. Then, they have to pay attention to less narcissistic individuals and to communicate by using the advertising messages which reconcile bought and dream products.

This study has several limits. First, this is not a longitudinal study, one can wonder how long do the reconcilable processes work? However, the reconcilable message is based on the means-end chain which links product attributes to consumers values. As individual values are enduring beliefs, one can expect that the reconcilable message is enduring. Second, this study focuses only on the personality of the consumer. It is likely that other individual characteristics may affect the gap between the bought and the dream processes. Third, this study is based on a convenience sample and the relations have been tested as regards only one product: cars.

Future researches have to complete this study in integrating characteristics which are easily usable in advertising, as socio-demographic criteria (income, gender, media exposure...). Then, it will be of managerial interest to determine the gap between dream and reality for the services and to find a possible compromise. For instance, the banking sectors the biggest advertiser. Thus, finding the advertisement which reconciles dream and reality of bank consumers will increase the efficiency of a global communication strategy.

APPENDIX 1

List of items

	Concrete Attributes		Abstract Attibutes
1	Shape/design	14	Aestheticism
2	Solidity/sturdiness	15	Comfort
3	Price	16	Road-holding
4	Colours	17	Brand prestige
5	Size	18	Brand originality
6	Consumption	19	Technological innovation
7	Options		
8	Availability		
9	Fuel type		
10	Braking		
11	Power		
12	Reliability		
13	Brand notoriety		
	Functional Consequences		**Psychosocial Consequences**
20	Easy handling	27	Feeling confident
21	Driving for pleasure	28	Feeling relaxed
22	Saving money	29	Escaping
23	Reducing the number of	30	Asserting oneself
24	accidents	31	Being noticed
25	Using the vehicle in all		
26	circumstances		
	Avoiding breakdowns		
	Being comfortably installed		
	Instrumental Values		**Terminal Values**
32	Self-controlled	41	Group-membership
33	Cheerful	42	Fulfilling oneself
34	Responsible	43	A sense of accomplishment
35	Capable	44	Self-respect
36	Dynamic	45	True friendship
37	Ambitious	46	Freedom
38	Respected	47	An exciting life
39	Clean	48	Happiness
40	Independent	49	Security
		50	Social recognition
		51	Pleasure

REFERENCES

Aaker, J. L. (1997). Dimensions of Brand Personality. *Journal of Marketing Research, 34*(3), 347-356.

Aurifeille, J. M. (1994). La Segmentation par les Chaînes Moyens-Fins: Concepts et Méthodes. *Cahier Cerege, 120*, I.A.E. de Poitiers.

Aurifeille, J. M. (1997). La Segmentation Moyens-Fins: Une Démarche Appliquée aux Comportements d'achat Alimentaire. *Economies et Sociétés, Développement agro-alimentaire, Série A.G., 23*(9), 117-146.

Aurifeille, J. M. (2000). A Bio-Mimetic Approach to Marketing Segmentation: Principles and Comparative Analysis. *European Journal of Economic and Social Systems, 14*(1), 93-108.

Aurifeille, J. M. (2004). Uncovering Consumers' Choice Processes: A Means-End Process Clustering (MPC) Method. *European Journal of Economics and Social Systems, 17*(1), 125- 145.

Aurifeille, J. M., and Jolibert, A., (1998). Des Valeurs Individuelles aux Comportements d'achat. In Presses académiques de l'Ouest, *Valeur, Marché et Organisation: Actes des XIVe Journées Internationales des IAE Nantes 1998*, 213-226.

Birdwell, A. E. (1968). A Study of the Influence of Image Congruence on Consumer Choice. *Journal of Business, 41* (January), 76-88.

FACIREM (2003). Logiciel de Collecte de Données Moyens-Fins QCMF (Questionnement de chaînes moyens-fins), Facirem, Université de la Réunion.

Ferrandi, J. M., Merunka, D., Valette-Florence, P., and De Barnier, V. (2002). Brand Personality: How Well Does a Human Personality Scale Apply to Brands?. *Asia Pacific Advances in Consumer Research, 5*, 53-60.

Freud, S. (1993). *Essais de Psychanalyse*. Petite Bibliothèque Payot. First published in German in 1920.

Gengler, C. E., and Reynolds, T. (1995). Consumer Understanding and Advertising Strategy: Analysis and Strategic Translation of Laddering Data. *Journal of Advertising Research, 35*(4), 19-33.

Gutman, J. (1982). A Means-End Chain Model Based on Consumer Categorization Processes. *Journal of Marketing, 46*(2), 60-72.

Gutman, J. (1984). Analysing Consumer Orientations Toward Beverages through Means-End Chain Analysis. *Psychology and Marketing, 1*(3/4), 23-43.

Hong, J. W., and Zinkhan, G. M. (1995). Self-Concept and Advertising Effectiveness; The Influence of Congruency, Conspicuousness, and Response Mode. *Psychology and Marketing, 12*(1), 53-77.

Horney, K. (1945). *Neurosis and Human Growth*. New-York–London: Norton.

Howard, J. A. (1994). *Buyer Behavior in Marketing Strategy*. Englewood Cliffs, New Jersey: Prentice Hall.

Kassarjian, H. H. (1971). Personality and Consumer Behavior: A Review. *Journal of Marketing Research, 8*(4), 409-418.

Kotler, P., and Dubois, B. (1997). *Kotler et Dubois Marketing Management, 9ème édition*. Publi Union.

Lee, D. H. (1990). Symbolic Interactionism: Some Implications for Consumer Self-Concept and Product Symbolism Research. *Advances in Consumer Research, 17*(1), 386-393.

Levy, S. J. (1959). Symbols for Sales. *Harvard Business Review, 37*(4), 117-124.

Manin, S., and Marde, S. (2003). La Validité des Protocoles de Collecte de Données Moyens-Fins Auto Administrés. Congrès de l'ACSEG.

Mizerski, R. W., and Settle, R. B. (1979). The Influence of Social Character on Preference for Social Versus Objective Infomation in Advertising. *Journal of Marketing Research, 16*(4), 552-558.

Olson, J. C., and Reynolds, T. (1983). Understanding Consumers' Cognitive Structures: Implications for Advertising Strategy. In L. Percy, and A. Woodside (Eds.), *Advertising and Consumer Psychology, (I),* (pp. 77-90). Lexington MA : Lexington Books.

Percy, L. (1988). The Often Subtle Linguistic Cues in Advertising. *Advances in Consumer Research, 15*(1), 269-274.

Plummer, J. T. (1984). How Personality Makes a Difference. *Journal of Advertising Research, 24*(6), 27-32.

Reynolds, T. J., Gengler, C. E., and Howard, D. J. (1995). A Means-End Analysis of Brand Persuasion Through Advertising. *International Journal of Research in Marketing, 12*(3), 257-266.

Reynolds, T .J., and Gutman, J. (1984a). Advertising is Image Management. *Journal of Advertising Research, 24*(1), 27-37.

Reynolds, T. J., Gutman, J., and Fiedler, J. A. (1984b). Understanding Consumer's Cognitive Structures: The Relationship of the Levels of Abstraction to Judgements of Psychological Distance and Preference. In A. Mitchell, and L. Alwitt (Eds.), *Psychological Processes of Advertising*

Effects: Theory, Research and Application (pp. 261-272). Hillsdale, NJ: Erlbaum.

Reynolds, T. J., and Jamieson, L. F. (1984c). Image Representations: An Analytical Framework in Perceived Quality of Products, Services and Stores. In J. Jacoby, and J. Olson (Eds.). (pp. 115-138), Lexington MA: Lexington Books.

Reynolds, T. J., and Gutman, J. (1988). Laddering Theory: Method, Analysis and Interpretation. *Journal of Advertising Research, 28*(1), 1-31.

Rokeach, M. (1973). *The Nature of Human Values.* New York: The Free Press.

Vinson, D. E., Scott, J. E., and Lamont, L. M. (1977). The Role of Personal Values in the Marketing and Consumer Behavior. *Journal of Marketing, 41*(2), 44-50.

Wang, C. L., and Mowen, J. C. (1997). The Separateness-Connectedness Self-Schema: Scale Development and Application to Message Construction. *Psychology and Marketing, 14*(2), 185-207.

Young, S., and Feigin, B. (1975). Using the Benefit Chain for Improved Strategy Formulation. *Journal of Marketing, 39*(3), 72-74.

In: Advertising
Editor: Evelyn P. Mann

ISBN 978-1-61324-679-5
© 2012 Nova Science Publishers, Inc.

Chapter 6

CHILDREN AND ADVERTISING: WHAT DO THEY THINK ABOUT ADVERTISEMENTS? HOW ARE THEY AFFECTED BY ADVERTISEMENTS?

Arzu Şener, Seval Güven and Ayfer Aydıner Boylu
Hacettepe University, Ankara, Turkey

ABSTRACT

In all circumstances television advertisements affect children of different age and gender groups in terms of consumption. Because of the ease to affect and lead children, advertisers consider them as the target audience. Today, since television advertisements have an important and effective role in the conscious raising of children who will be socialized as the consumers of the future, we are confronted by the imperative to focus on television ads. For this reason, this study has been planned and conducted with the aim of determining the effects of television advertisements on primary school age children and understanding their attitude towards advertisements. The sample of this research is constituted by 225 students, who are selected by random sampling method from the 6th, 7th and 8th grades of 5 primary schools within Ankara city territories. The results of the research show that girls watch more television advertisements than boys do ($p<.05$) and that the ratio of those who "always" watch television advertisements, decline with the increase in education level. Furthermore, at the end of the research it was found that children, be it a girl or a boy at any education level, want to possess the goods and services that they see on television advertisements. However, it was also seen that there is a high ratio of those who think that goods and services that they purchase sometimes carry the characteristics stated in the advertisements. Moreover, the findings of the research also indicate that while most of the children agree with the fact that advertisements are "entertaining" and "effective in shopping," a considerable number of children think that advertisements cause prodigality. More critical than that, findings pinpoint that the ratio of those who think that advertisements are "honest and real" decline while the ratio (p<.05) of those who think that advertisements are "misguiding and deceptive" increase with the increase in grade level.

INTRODUCTION

Change and progress are experienced in all areas around the world. Especially, the increase in literacy rate that came along with industrialization and the growing importance of media in our lives lead to changes in the society's needs and values (Güven, 1996). This structural change in the society and developments in the world have been influential in the economic sector as well. As the basic elements of economic life, managements have various goals like increasing sales, introducing products and services, informing the consumer, enabling the consumer to purchase goods or services in line with their desires and needs, creating and strengthening a brand or a brand image (Bayraktaroğlu 1999; Bir and Maviş, 1988). It is evident that managements want to fulfill these goals. Nevertheless, the eventual increase in goods and services parallel with the changes and developments in economy and technology increased the gap between the producer and the consumer and also perpetuated the competition among producers (Bir and Maviş, 1988). Together with the increased competition, reasons like raising consumer awareness, evaluation of the consumers' time and money, the need to inform the consumers in the internal and foreign markets augment the importance of communication in marketing (Bayraktaroğlu, 1999; Dalbudak and Zorman, 2000). Marketing communication carries the goal to publicize the company, product, idea or service of the company to the consumer, customer or to the public (Budak, 2001). If the consumer does not know the product, its price or where that product can be bought, it is not possible for the company to sell it. Therefore, the costumer should be informed about the product, price and distribution channels. This can be realized by promotion efforts within marketing communication methods (Bayraktaroğlu, 1999). Promotion efforts can be explained as a function informing and persuading the consumer as well as affecting their decision in buying (Kurtz and Boone, 1987). Advertisement as a promotion effort is preferred since it provides mass communication (Bayraktaroğlu, 1999; Güzel, 2001). Although many people perceive advertising as new and immature, within the dynamism of free market it has become a significant sector which can use aesthetic elements to motivate the consumer and form communication in a shorter way (Çetinkaya, 1993). Equipped with such functions, today advertising is one of the most crucial cultural factors shaping and reflecting our lives. It is an inevitable part of everybody's lives at all places. Even if newspapers are not read, or television is not watched it is not possible to escape images that dominate the urban space. Therefore, today advertising has an autonomous superstructure which encompasses the media and which has no limits (Yulafçı, 2000). The beginning of exchange among people coincides with the same historical process in which advertising is born. Advertising in our country first appeared in newspapers and magazines that came out in the second half of the 18th century. However, advertising through newspapers and magazines did not grasp much attraction due to low literacy rate among the public (Suna, 1963). While advertisements became widespread in radio broadcasting in the 1950s, their most active and influential form appeared in the 1970s when television entered into our lives (Öztürk, 1996; Özyurt, 2004; RTÜK, 2004; Ünsal, 2000). Regardless of the short history of advertising in Turkey, on a general scale advertising fulfills functions like creating demand for a product or service, increasing that demand or performing other demand methods. Since advertising carries out these goals on a large scale with its ability to reach great masses, it is also called "mass sale." Advertisement, as a communication tool, informs people about the benefits of a product or service and persuades them. These constitute the functions of advertising (Bayraktaroğlu, 1999; Dalbudak and Zorman, 2000; Güven, 1996). The first and the most important function of advertisement is "to inform individuals." The assumption that all consumers in the market have the whole and real knowledge of products and services in the market is an invalid assumption. The rational consumer starts to seek information on the product and service when she decides to meet her wishes and needs. This search for information requires time and energy for the consumer. In such a case, the individual tries to reduce the cost for gaining information and leans towards advertisements which can give information with low costs (Dalbudak and Zorman, 2000; Filizer, 1999). In fact, modern marketing -the father of advertising- aims at understanding and determining customer wishes and needs. Accordingly, it also aspires to develop products in line with these needs and to present the product by announcing the product's availability through advertisements (Dalbudak and Zorman, 2000). The second function of advertising is to "persuade the consumer", i.e. to try to make the consumer choose the product which have been advertised. The function of persuasion is the main goal of contemporary modern advertising (Dalbudak and Zorman 2000; Filizer, 1999). Advertisers benefit from the persuasion power of advertisement in the light of social values, because consumers give importance not only to rational and objective criteria like price, quality, and endurance, but also to emotional criteria like color, prestige, fashionability. As a result, there can appear problems such as introducing groundless assertions about the product, directing the consumer to purchase products that are not needed and misusing the consumer's inexperience and lack of knowledge (Brettman, 1979; Kavas, 1985). Each and every individual living in the society is a "consumer." In order to maintain their lives, people have to meet some needs like nutrition, clothing, sheltering, leisure and entertainment. As a result of this, consumption appears as a mere economic concept. According to our contemporary value judgments, consumption is seen to be one of the most vital ways of existence. Thus, everything becomes meaningful in terms of consumption. However, every product and service starts to dissatisfy people at the very moment they are consumed. In turn, people lean towards more consumption. Therefore, consumption oriented life style is being set down and societies transform into consumption societies. In due course, consumers cannot only behave like *homo economicus*. They also give importance to emotional criteria (color, prestige, fashionability and etc.) along with objective criteria (price, quality, endurance and etc.). The significance attributed to emotional criteria as well as objective criteria and the constant instinct to consume oblige advertisers to use the power of persuasion in the light of social value judgments (Dalbudak and Zorman, 2000; Fromm, 1982; Kavas, 1998).

In line with the fact that consumption is not a mere economic concept, today advertising sector concentrates on perpetuating the attitude and behavior of consumer towards a product, service or idea by using creative ability rather than merely informing and entertaining the consumers (Budak, 2001; Dalbudak and Zorman, 2000; Mattelard, 1992). Within this consumption society, it is evident that the consumer contribution and dominance in the modern economy are increasing everyday. This dominance becomes more visible with the increase of consumer income level and at the same time with the increase of goods and services in quantity and quality. In the first place, the aim of producers and sellers is to make consumers purchase their goods and services. In order to persuade consumers, these producers develop methods like advertising, individual sales, exhibitions, free samples, coupons, flyers, trade fairs and packaging products. These methods have been utilized in order to transform the society into a consumer society, to shape and settle this consumer society. Still, the most effective method is advertising, especially advertising through mass communication (Gönen and Özgen, 1988; Mattelard, 1992; Pira and Sohodol, 2004). Means of mass communication can be in written, visual or auditory format. While they may contain all these characteristics by themselves, sometimes they may have only a few of these characteristics. As television provides both visual and auditory stimulus (message), it is the most effective means of mass communication (Atay and Öncü, 2003). Along with this, the existence of at least one colored television at each home regardless of its socio-economic level and an average of 5-6 hours spent for watching television caused advertisers to use television effectively for introducing and selling products or services (Aksoy and Batmaz, 1995; Dalbudak and Zorman, 2000; Filizer, 1999; Kulen, 1990; Mete, 2004; Özgen, 1989; Öztürk, 1996; Suna, 1963; Turan, 1996; Yengin, 1994). Thus, despite the short history of television in Turkey, it has become widely used and indispensible for various sections of the society within a short period of time.

Television has the power of affecting individuals as a whole. This influence is seen the most in individual's behavior concerning consumption (Öztürk, 1996). "Mass culture," which is pioneered by television, became a mass culture that is known, embraced and used by all world societies at the end of the 20th century. Television is more effective on individuals especially in consumption societies, because of the fact that individuals are interested in televisions and broadcasting due to economic, social and cultural reasons (Cereci, 1996). When we look at general ratings of television broadcastings, it is evident that although the ratings of television advertisements are the lowest, their immediate affectivity is high. Television advertisements have the purpose of creating change in the attitude of target audience towards the products or services produced by companies. Thus, mostly the focus is on "introduction and selling" (Bovee and Arens, 1986; Cereci, 1996; Dalbudak and Zorman, 2000; Kocabaş, Elden and Yurdakul, 2000; Rutherford, 1998). The reactions given by an adult or a child to television advertisements reflect what that individual feels about the instinct to purchase that product (Devrez, 1979; Kocabaş, Elden and Yurdakul, 2000). Such reactions are not caused by methods of pressure but rather by the method of enticement. This enticement, which cannot be realized in the beginning, becomes more visible and faster as the ages of individuals get younger (Çiğdem and Dikeçligil, 1991; Özdiker,

2004). To put in other words, since children are more vulnerable to deception and orientation due to their inexperience, they cannot evaluate advertisements objectively (Akbulut, 2004; Aker, 1978; Kocabaş and Kocabaş, 2004). For this reason advertisements affect children more easily. Besides, teenagers and children have more determinate roles in giving decisions about consumption (Buckingham, 1993). Hence, most of the new consumption tools conduct market researches and activities oriented towards children and teenagers (Akçalı, 2004; Özgen, 1995), because now more teenagers and children are included in the economy as consumers. In our contemporary society, children can give decisions on and perform the process of purchasing. Today, not only can children express their desires and needs clearly, but also they can be very insistent on their parents in the process of buying. Therefore, unlike their coevals before they direct consumption behaviors of families even if they do not purchase by themselves. As a matter of fact, some studies underline an increase in the consumption expenditures of 82% of families who go shopping with their children (Gürel, 2004; Kaner, 1989). As for the children's decision in buying, mostly advertisements are used as a source of information. Thus, advertisements can influence children to a large extend (Dalbudak and Zorman, 2000; Halloran et al., 1973; Kapferer, 1991; Kocabaş, Elden and Yurdakul, 2000; Pira and Sohodol, 2004; Tokgöz, 1982). Children are constantly confronted with materialist values through television advertisements; thus, advertisements have great effects on the children's thought systems. It is a fact that children gain basic categories that shape social experiences through advertisements. By exploiting children's curiosities through wrong and deceiving methods, television advertisements increase consumption of various products. Therefore, it is plausible to suggest that specific techniques used in advertisements can be deceiving and misguiding for the children who cannot evaluate advertisements adequately. Confrontation with television advertisements for a long time can cause changes in children's values, attitude and behaviors. According to some observations, when a child sees another child, just like himself, praising a product or service, his instinct of imitation gets stronger. Therefore, he can be easily influenced by the advertisement and wants to possess the products in that advertisement (Öztürk, 1996; Kaner, 1989). In fact, the findings of Tokgöz's (1980) research show that children are pushed toward consumption through the effects of advertisements. Similarly, in a study conducted by Robinson et.al. (2001), a special program was organized for some children of 8-9 years. This program, which also included parents, aimed at reducing the time children spend for watching television. In due course, children's watching television was restricted incrementally under the control of their families and they were encouraged to engage with other activities. After this procedure, a 70% decline was found in children's demands for toys. In order for the children to be influenced by advertisements, first of all they have to get some information from advertisements and then they have to evaluate and interpret them. Self characteristics like age and gender, social atmosphere and the way the advertisement is presented are of the important factors guiding this process (Turan, 1996). Beginning from the age of 2, children can comprehend everything in their environments (Aksoy and Batmaz, 1995). In between the age range of 0-4, the child leads his family towards consumption covertly. This concealed force becomes visible in his behaviors as he gets older (Filizer, 1999). Moreover, while children of 4-5 years undertake the role of consumers, at the ages of 9-10 they start to differentiate between television programs and advertisements and thus, they become conscious consumers. At the age of 12, they join the society as consumers (Aksoy and Batmaz, 1995; Filizer, 1999).

However, the effects of advertisements on children vary not only according to age, but also in relation with gender. Children in the same age group can show differences in consumption behavior in relation to their gender differences (Rutherford, 1998). Tokgöz's (1982) study point out that there are gender differences in learning consumption skills of the children in the same age group. For instance, girls like the music and dances in the advertisements. On the other hand, boys remember television advertisements more than the girls do. In addition to that, there are also differences between the kinds of advertisements watched by girls and boys. To be more specific, while girls watch advertisements about cleaning and banks, boys watch advertisements about toys more. Regardless of age and gender differences, advertisements affect children in terms of consumption behaviors. Because of the ease to affect and lead children in the consumption society, advertisers consider them as the target audience (Aksoy and Batmaz, 1995; Uebert, Meare and Davidson, 1973). Television advertisements constitute a new dimension for experience and socialization in Turkey and in the world for everyone regardless of their ages. It is evident that in Turkey television is very effective for accepting and forming new social values in the newly emerging generation. Accordingly, since television advertisements have an important and effective role in the conscious raising of children who will be socialized as the consumers of the future, today we are confronted by the imperative to focus on television advertisements. Another reason for the specific focus on television advertisements stems from the fact that among the mass communication tools, children use mostly television. Advertisements squeezed within television programs lead children to consume more by affecting them in terms of both quality and quantity. Here, it should be kept in mind that children begin to participate actively in consumption starting from the age of 12 and they also guide their families' consumption patterns. Thus, more studies that investigate the effects of advertisements on children and how children regard this issue should be conducted. Following this need, this study has been planned and conducted with the aim of determining the effects of television advertisements on primary school age children and understanding their attitude towards advertisements.

METHODOLOGY

Sample

The 6th, 7th and 8th grade students constitute the universe of this research. As the research area, 5 primary schools were chosen from the districts of Bahçelievler, Dikmen, Elvankent, Natoyolu and İncirli within Ankara city borders. 45 students were chosen from the 6th, 7th and 8th grades of each of these five schools within the research scope. Therefore, N=225 has been reached (Çıngı, 1994). Research data were gathered through face-to-face interviews basing on a survey form.

Evaluation and Analysis of the Data

The evaluation of the data gathered at the end of the research was done through x^2 analysis in the SPSS 12 program. When there are values less than 5 within the expected frequency in the crosstabs, the value of Likelihood Ratio is taken into consideration (Çıngı, 1994).

FINDINGS AND DISCUSSION

General Information on Children

More than the half of the children (52%) within the scope of the study is boys, whereas 48% of the children consist of girls. In this sample, while children in the "13 age" group occupy the first rank with a ratio of 32.9%, the ratio of students continuing in the $6^{th}, 7^{th}, 8^{th}$ grades is the same (33.3%).

The Situation of Children's Watching Television

Television is the most widely used means of mass communications. When it is recognized that rural or urban, rich or poor, more or less educated, everyone has a television, then the effects of television on children's lives are better understood (Lindstrom and Seybold, 2003; Arslan, 2004). In fact, television may become the most crucial tool that brings the external world into the home for the children, especially during infancy period and the years after (Güler, 1989). For example, according to a study conducted by the International Children's Center, children of 2 ages know how to turn on the television and when they turn into the age of 3, they start to stare at television everyday (Revue, 1998).

More than the half of the children in the scope of this research (56.9%) stated that they "always" watch television. While 41.3% of the children expressed that they "sometimes" watch television, the ratio of those who said that they "never" watch television (%1.8) is quite low (Table 1). In a research carried out in 15 countries in the continents of Europe, Asia and South America along with the USA, it was found that children watch television almost everyday (Lindstrom and Seybold, 2003).

Table 1. The Case of Children's Watching Television

Explanatory Variables		The Situation of Watching Television							
		Always		Sometimes		Never		Total	
		n	%	n	%	n	%	n	%
Gender	Female	59	54.6	48	44.4	1	0.9	108	100.0
	Male	69	59.0	45	38.5	3	2.6	117	100.0
	Total	128	56.9	93	41.3	4	1.8	225	100.0
LR = 1.565 p>.05 df= 2									
Grade	6th grade	42	56.0	33	44.0	-	-	75	100.0
	7th grade	46	61.3	28	37.3	1	13.0	75	100.0
	8th grade	40	53.3	32	42.7	3	4.0	75	100.0
	Total	128	56.9	93	41.3	4	1.8	225	100.0
LR = 5.552 p>.05 df= 4									

As for Turkey, the ratio of watching television is increasing gradually. Thanks to the new wave of series and soap operas, Turkey caught up with the USA and now she is in the first rank in terms of the ratio of watching television. Furthermore, the high ratio of those children who stated that they "always" watch television in this research signifies the high frequency of watching television among primary school age children.

When this issue is analyzed on the basis of gender difference, it is seen that the ratio of boys who state that they "always" watch television (59.0%) is higher than the ratio of the girls who "always" watch television (54.6%) (Table 1). This finding reflects upon the judgment that boys watch television more than the girls do. Regarded the issue on the basis of education level, it is found that in each of the three grades more than the half of the children expressed that they "always" watch television (6th grade: 56.0%, 7th grade: 61.3%, 8th grade: 53.3%) (Table 1)

The Average Time Children Spend Everyday for Watching Television

As the most widely used means of mass communication which provides both visual and auditory stimuli, television has penetrated into children's lives. As a matter of fact, a child spends more time in front of the television than he spends for reading or playing games (Atay and Öncü, 2003; Doğan, 2003).

Table 2. The Average Time Children Spend Everyday for Watching Television

Explanatory Variables		Time spent for Watching Television								
		0 – 2 hours		3-4 hours		5-6 hours		7+ hours		Total	
		n	%	n	%	n	%	N	%	n	%
Gender	Female	38	35.2	53	49.1	17	15.7	-	-	108	100.0
	Male	46	39.3	50	42.7	20	17.9	1	0.9	117	100.0
	Total	84	37.3	103	45.8	37	16.4	1	0.4	225	100.0
LR = 2.120 p>.05 df= 3											
Grade	6th grade	29	38.7	35	46.7	10	13.3	1	1.3	75	100.0
	7th grade	24	32.0	36	48.0	15	20.0	-	-	75	100.0
	8th grade	31	41.3	32	42.7	12	16.0	-	-	75	100.0
	Total	84	37.3	103	45.8	37	16.4	1	0.4	225	100.0
LR = 5.175 p>.05 df= 6											

45.8 % of the children within the scope of the study watch television for "3-4 hours" in average a day, whereas 37.3% watch television for "0-2 hours" in average. Only 16.4% expressed that they watch television for "5-6 hours" in average. At the same time, the ratio of those who watch television "0-2 hours" and "3-4 hours" a day (81.3%) cannot be undervalued (Table 2). When the length of the advertisements seen during this period of watching television, it can be argued that advertisements can affect children in shaping and guiding their consumption behaviors. In a study carried out by Revue (1998) in France, it was found that 30% of the children watch television for 3 hours and 28 minutes a day. When the issue is examined in terms of gender difference, it is observed that about half of the girls (49.1%) and 42.7% of boys watch television for "3-4 hours" a day in average (Table 2). This finding is also illuminated by a research conducted by Saatçiler (1997). The research pointed out that 40% of boys watch television for more than 3 hours, whereas 40% of girls watch television for only 2-3 hours. Analyzed in terms of grades in which children continue their education, in all grades those who watch television for "3-4 hours" a day in average occupy the first rank (6th grade: 46.7%; 7th grade: 48.0 %, 8th grade: 42.7%). Those who express watching television for "0-2 hours" a day in average (6th grade: 38.7%, 7th grade: 32.0%, 8th grade: 41.3%) follow the first rank (Table 2). On the other hand, in a study conducted by Revue (1998) in France, it is found that children of 11-14 ages watch television for 2 hours 1 minute. This difference between research findings might be stemming from the fact that these researches were conducted at different times in different cultures.

The Situation of Children's Watching Television Advertisements

Children start to watch television almost at the time of birth. Since grasping ideas from television does not require any skills, they became a significant part of the advertising watchers at early ages. Considering the role that television has in extending the limits of consumption, children turn into a crucial target for advertising industry. In the light of this goal, children are exposed to thousands of advertisements every year (Unnikrishnan and Baipai, 1996; Leonhardt and Kathleen, 1997; Moore and Lutz, 2000, Kunkel et al., 2004). According to a study carried out in England, a child watches around 140.000 advertisements until he turns into 18 (Lindstorm and Seybold, 2003). In our study, it is seen that those who "sometimes" watch advertisements (66.7 %) are predominant, while the ratio of those who "always" watch advertisements is 27.1 % (Table 3). Being the most important factor affecting the family's decision in buying, children gradually became the focus for advertisers (Mengü and Karadogan, 2003). As mentioned before, while children are related to products about themselves, now they watch around twenty thousand advertisements in a year (Gürel, 2004). As such, they became the target of a wide array of products. By using action, music, cartoon heroes, rhymed mottos and child heroes, advertisers have actually found the ways to attract children's attention more (Cesur and Paker, 2007). It can be argued that such attempts of advertisers are successful, because as our study also indicates the ratio of those who "never" watch television are only 6.2% and; thus, the tendency of children to watch television advertisements are necessarily high.

The ratio of girls who "sometimes" watch television advertisements are higher than those of boys (female: 73.2% male: 60.7 %). While the ratio of girls who "never" watch television advertisements is 1.9 %, this ratio is found to be 10.3 % for boys (P < .05) (Table 3). When the issue is analyzed in terms of grades in which children receive education, it is seen that more than the half of the 6th graders (58.7%), 62.7 % of 7th graders and majority of the 8th graders (78.7 %) "sometimes" watch television advertisements. Children who express watching television "always" declines with the level of education, whereas the ratio of those who "sometimes" watch television increases with the increase in education level (always: 6th grads: 33.3 %, 7th grade: 29.3 %, 8th grade: 18.7 %; sometimes: 6th grade: 58.7 %, 7th grade: 62.7 %, 8th grade: 78.7 %) (Table 3). This situation might be interpreted as children are less interested in television advertisements as they grow up due to socialization as consumers.

Table 3. The Case of Children's Watching Television Advertisements

Explanatory Variables		The Case of Watching Television Advertisements							
		Always		Sometimes		Never		Total	
		n	%	n	%	n	%	n	%
Gender	Female	27	25.0	79	73.2	2	1.9	108	100.0
	Male	34	29.1	71	60.7	12	10.3	117	100.0
	Total	61	27.1	150	66.7	14	6.2	225	100.0
X2 = 8.026 p<.05 df= 2									
Grades	6th grade	25	33.3	44	58.7	6	8.0	75	100.0
	7th grade	22	29.3	47	62.7	6	8.0	75	100.0
	8th grade	14	18.7	59	78.7	2	2.7	75	100.0
	Total	61	27.1	150	66.7	14	6.2	225	100.0
LR = 8.849 p>.05 df= 4									

As a matter of fact, there have been studies which showed that children's behavior concerning television advertisements are connected to the development of their perceptive skills.

Therefore, these studies pinpoint that as children become capable of differentiating the reality from imaginary, they start to be less attentive to advertisements (Van Evra, 1998).

Types of Advertisements that Children Watch the Most

Marketers use television as a means of communication which can reach to children at an earlier age than printed media can reach. Around 80 % of children oriented advertisements concentrate on toys, breakfast cereals, candies and fast food restaurants (Kunkel and Gantz, 1992).

Therefore, most of the advertisements created for children are about food. On the contrary, in this research more than the half of the children in question (52.9 %) pinpointed "car advertisements" as the most viewed kind of advertisement.

The reason for that lies in the fact that 52.0 % of the children within the scope of the research consists of male students. Furthermore, this study has also underlined the finding that the ratio of those who stated watching "advertisements on personal care products" (44.4 %) and the ratio of those who expressed watching "advertisements on food" (44.0 %) are equal and in the second place.

The least viewed advertisement among children is "technological products" (5.3 %) which is preceded by advertisements about toys (19.1 %) (Table 4). Koç et.al. (1998) conducted a research which investigated how students of different socio-economic levels are affected by television advertisements.

The findings of this study suggested that children remember advertisements related to "food" and "personal care products" the most. This might stem from the fact that these advertisements are watched more.

Table 4. Types of Advertisements that Children Watch the Most

Explanatory Variables		Types of Advertisements that Children Watch the Most														
		Toys Advertisements		Car Advertisements		Bank Advertisements		Clothings Advertisements		Food Advertisements		Personal Care Products Advertisements		Credit Card Advertisements		Technological products like mobile phones, computers etc. Advertisements
		n	%	n	%	N	%	n	%	n	%	n	%	n	%	n	%
Gender	Female (n=108)	24	22.2	22	20.4	25	23.1	58	53.7	52	48.1	78	72.2	19	17.6	6	5.6
	Male (n=117)	19	16.2	97	82.9	45	38.5	34	29.1	47	40.2	22	18.8	51	43.6	6	5.1
	Total (n=225)	43	19.1	119	52.9	70	31.1	92	40.9	99	44.0	100	44.4	70	31.1	12	5.3
Grade	6th grade (n=75)	24	32.0	36	48.0	20	26.7	33	44.0	38	50.7	31	41.3	19	25.3	3	4.0
	7th grade (n=75)	12	16.0	42	56.0	27	36.0	27	36.0	32	42.7	29	38.7	23	30.7	8	10.7
	8th grade (n=75)	7	9.3	41	54.7	23	30.7	32	42.7	29	38.7	40	53.3	28	37.3	1	1.3
	Total (n=225)	43	19.1	119	52.9	70	31.1	92	40.9	99	44.0	100	44.4	70	31.1	12	5.3

$X^2=1.300$ p>.05 df= 1 $X^2=88.144$ p<.05 df=1 $X^2=6.145$ p<.05 df= 1 $X^2=14.111$ p<.05 df= 1 $X^2=1.450$ p>.05 df=1 $X^2=64.904$ p<.05 df=1
$X^2=17.710$ p<.05 df= 1 $X^2=0.020$ p>.05 df= 1

$X^2=13.442$ p<.05 df= 2 $X^2=1.451$ p>.05 df= 2 $X^2=2.012$ p>.05 df=23 $X^2=0.982$ p>.05 df=23 $X^2=2.705$ p>.05 df=2 $X^2=3.769$ p>.05 df= 2
$X^2=3.138$ p>.05 df=2
LR =6.710 p<.05 df= 2

Table 5. Elements in Advertisements which Children Find Attractive

Explanatory Variables		Elements Which are Found to be Attractive in Advertisements														
		Music		Voice		Image		Advertisement Actors		Text		Effects		All		None
		N	%	n	%	n	%	n	%	N	%	n	%	n	%	n	%
Gender	Female (n=108)	68	63.0	26	24.1	52	48.1	48	44.4	33	30.6	1	0.9	45	41.7	1	0.9
	Male (n=117)	44	37.6	41	35.0	53	45.3	42	35.9	27	23.1	3	2.7	43	36.8	4	3.4
	Total (n=225)	112	49.8	67	29.8	105	46.7	90	40.0	60	26.7	4	1.8	88	39.1	5	2.2

$X^2=13.442$ p<.05 df= 2 $X^2=1.451$ p>.05 df= 2 $X^2=2.012$ p>.05 df=23 $X^2=0.982$ p>.05 df=23 $X^2=2.705$ p>.05 df= 2 $X^2=3.769$ p>.05 df= 2 LR =3.138 p>.05 df= 2 LR =6.710 p<.05 df= 2

Explanatory Variables		Music		Voice		Image		Advertisement Actors		Text		Effects		All		None
Grade	6th grade (n=75)	41	54.7	26	34.7	34	45.3	32	42.7	22	29.3	1	1.3	27	36.0	1	1.3
	7th grade (n=75)	38	50.7	21	28.0	36	48.0	30	40.0	20	26.7	3	4.0	31	41.3	2	2.7
	8th grade (n=75)	33	44.0	20	26.7	35	46.7	28	37.3	18	24.0	-		30	40.0	2	2.7
	Total (n=225)	112	5.3	67	29.8	105	4.7	90	40.0	60	26.7	4	1.8	88	39.1	5	2.2

$X^2=13.442$ p<.05 df= 2 $X^2=1.451$ p>.05 df= 2 $X^2=2.012$ p>.05 df= 2 $X^2=0.982$ p>.05 df=23 $X^2=2.705$ p>.05 df=23 $X^2=3.769$ p>.05 df= 2 LR =3.138 p>.05 df= 2 LR =6.710 p<.05 df= 2

Among girls, the most watched advertisement type is "personal care advertisements" with a ratio of 72.2 %, whereas this ratio is found to be 18.8 % for boys. The majority of the boys (82.9 %) stated "car advertisements" as the most watched advertisement type. Besides, the fact that 43.6 % of the boys and only 17.6 % of the girls watch "credit card advertisements" might be interpreted as boys' being more interested in advertisements about services (Table 4). Thus, it has been detected that there is a significant statistical relationship between gender and watching different types of advertisements like car, bank, clothing, personal care products and credit cards (P<.05).

When the subject is analyzed in relation to the grades levels, the findings show that around the half of the 6th graders (50.7%) state "food advertisements" as the most watched advertisements type. On the other hand, students of 7th and 8th grades mentioned "car advertisements" as the most viewed advertisement kind (7th grade: 56.0 %, 8th grade: 54.7 %). As the grade level increases the ratio of those who state watching "toys advertisements" and "food advertisements" decline (P<.05) (toys advertisements: 6th grade: 32.0 %, 7th grade: 16.0 %, 8th grade: 9.3 %; food advertisements: 6th grade: 50.7%, 7th grade: 42.7 %, 8th grade: 38.7 %) (Table 4). This finding indicates that as the children grow up, their interest in toys and attractive foods decrease.

Elements in Advertisements Which Children Find Attractive

The results of the research point out that the children within the scope of this study find "music" (49.8 %) as the most attractive element in television advertisements. This ratio is followed by "images" with 46.7 % and "advertisement actors" with a ratio of 40.0 %. While 39.1 % of children affirm that they find "every" element in television advertisements attractive, the ratio of those who state that they find "none" of the advertisements attractive is quite low (2.2%). In other words, majority of the children find at least one element of advertisements attractive (Table 5).

In Koç et.al's (1988) study, the forms of presenting advertisements (elements, music, song, dance) are effective in making the recollection of advertisements easier. Similarly, Karaca et.al's (2007) study findings show that children are most affected by advertisements in which movie-cartoon heroes and children take part and which has good music.

In our study, among girls, the most attractive element in television advertisements is "music" (63.0%) (P<.05). Although among boys, "image" (45.3 %) takes the first rank as the most attractive element, still the ratio of girls stating image as the most attractive element (48.1 %) is higher than boys (45.3 %). This result arouses an impression of girls giving more importance to image and music than the boys do.

When the issue is analyzed in terms of grade levels in which children continue their education, the findings of the research pinpoint that students in the 6th grades (54.7 %) and 7th grades (50.7%) who indicate "music" is the most attractive element in advertising take the lead. This is followed by those who give the answer of "image" (6th grads: 45.3 %, 7th grade: 48.0%). In the 8th grade, while the ratio of students who find "image" (46.7 %) as the most attractive element occupies the first rank, the second place belongs to those stating "music" (44.4%) as the most attractive element.

As it can be seen in Table 7, as the education level increases, children's attention on advertisement actors, music (P<.05), voice and text starts to decay gradually. This situation might be caused by the fact that as children grow up, there is also an increase in their ability to differentiate between the constructed image and the people who try to impose these images on them.

The Situation of Children Wanting to Possess the Goods and Services Seen on Advertisements

Being presented to the children with amazing visual and audio effects, advertisements arouse consumptions instincts of children and thus activate their feeling of possession. This situation increases children's tendency to consume, so it transforms children into consumption slaves. Children of all families, regardless of their education and cultural levels, get their share from the ruthless concussions of television advertisements (Arslan, 2004).

The majority of the children (72.0 %) "sometimes" want to have the goods or services seen on television advertisements. On the other hand, the ratio of those who "always" want to possess the goods or services seen on television advertisements is 24.0 % (Table 6).

As a matter of fact, Koç et.al's (1988) study found that 38.0% of children absolutely believe in the need to buy the thing on television advertisements, whereas 52% stated that some of these could be bought. Still, 10.0 % of children expressed that everything seen on television advertisements could be bought.

Many studies point out that advertisements constitute an important source of children demands on products (Robinson et al., 2001; Robertson et. al., 1989; Devrez, 1979; AC Nielsen Zet, 1999; Buijzen and Valkenburg, 2003a;

Caron and Ward, 1975; Robertson and Rossiter, 1973; Goldberg,1990; Gorn and Goldberg ,1977; Yavas and Abdul-Gader, 1993; Elden and Ulukök, 2006; Arslan, 2004; Jensen, 1995; Williams and Veeck, 1998; Holdert and Antonides, 1997; Ahuja and Stinson, 1993.; Dunne, 1999). For instance, in a research conducted by Robinson et.al (2001), the findings indicate that the frequency of children's toys demands is 70 % less in children who watch television and advertisements less. In another study carried out by Robertson et.al. (1989) it was found that television advertisements enhance unnecessary consumption desires of children. Likewise, Devrez's (1979) study showed that advertisements create a desire for buying the products that are seen on advertisements.

In addition to these, AC Nielsen Zet (1999) organized a research in order to determine to what extend the advertisements are effective in children's and teenagers' buying and decisions on brands.

In this study, which included 2000 families, it was shown that 82.0% of families who go shopping with their children increase their spending in line with the wishes of their children. Thus, it was found that children constitute a leading force in buying.

Gender also has an important role affecting the demand of the product which is advertised. While majority of the girls (80.6 %) "sometimes" want to have to goods seen on television advertisements, this ratio is 64.1 % for boys. In line with this finding, it can be asserted that girls want to possess the good or services they see on television advertisements more than the boys do. This situation makes us think that girls use television advertisements as means of socialization more and they are more affected by these advertisements.

Moreover, it can also be argued that their great interest in personal care products, due to their ages, lead advertisers to create more advertisements on these products.

On the other hand, studies show that boys are more insistent on buying products seen on television advertisements more than the girls (Ward and Wackamn, 1972; Sheikh ad Moleski, 1977). The divergence between research findings might stem from cultural and historical differences of researches' scopes.

Still, a statistically significant relationship was found between the situation of wanting to possess the goods or services seen on television advertisements and gender (P<.05).

Table 6. The Situation of Children Wanting to Possess the Goods and Services Seen On Advertisements

Explanatory Variables		The Situation of Children Wanting to Possess the Goods and Services Seen On Advertisements							
		Always		Sometimes		Never		Total	
		N	%	n	%	n	%	N	%
Gender	Female	20	18.5	87	80.6	1	0.9	108	100.0
	Male	34	29.1	75	64.1	8	6.8	117	100.0
	Total	54	24.0	162	72.0	9	4.0	225	100.0
LR = 10.399 p<.05 df= 2									
Grade	6th grade	18	24.0	56	74.7	1	1.3	75	100.0
	7th grade	17	22.7	54	72.0	4	5.3	75	100.0
	8th grade	19	25.3	52	69.3	4	5.3	75	100.0
	Total	54	24.0	162	72.0	9	4.0	225	100.0
LR = 2.659 p>.05 df= 4									

Other than gender difference education level is also poignant in determining the demand of the product seen on television advertisements. Generally speaking, it was found that as the grade level in which children receive education increase, children's demand on products or services seen on television advertisements decreases (always: 6th grade: 24.0%, 7th grade: 22.7 %, 8th grade: 25.3 %; sometimes: 6th grade: 74.7 %, 8th grade: 69.3 %) (Table 6). This result might signify that the ratio of children affected by advertisements decline as they grow up.

Thus, being exposed to advertisements is a necessary precondition for developing a cognitive defense against the persuasive influence of advertisements. This argument can also backed by the results of many studies which show that the effects of advertisements on children decrease as children grow up and; thus, the demands of children for advertised products decline as well (Buijzen and Valkenburg, 2003b; Ward and Wackman, 1972; Robertson and Rossiter, 1974; Ward, Wackman and Wartella, 1977; Barry and Hansen, 1973; Bever et al., 1975; Mitchell, 1986; Galst and White, 1976; Lewis and Hill, 1998; Moore and Lutz, 2000; Valkenburg, 2000; Young, 2003; North and Kotze, 2001).

For example, in a study conducted by Robertson and Rossiter (1974) it was found that demanding the advertised products decline with the increase in grade level.

Table 7. Reasons Behind Children's Wanting to Possess the Goods or Services Seen on Advertisements

Explanatory Variables		Reasons for Wanting to Possess the Goods or Services Seen on Advertisements									
		Liking the product or services seen on advertisements		Liking the advertisements of product or services		Only curiosity		Wanting to be like actors seen on advertisements		Wanting to possess just because other friends possess.	
		N	%	n	%	n	%	n	%	n	%
Gender	Female (n=108)	68	63.0	27	25.0	47	43.5	20	18.5	1	0.9
	Male (n=117)	71	60.7	40	34.2	59	50.4	16	13.7	4	3.4
	Total (n=225)	139	61.8	67	29.8	106	47.1	36	16.0	5	2.2

X^2=0.124 p>.05 df=1 X^2=2.267 p>.05 df= 1 X^2= 1.076 p>.05 df= 1 X^2=0.980 p>.05 df= 1
LR =1.731 p>.05 df= 1

Grade											
Grade	6th grade (n=75)	45	60.0	22	29.3	37	49.3	20	26.7	3	4.0
	7th grade (n=75)	45	60.0	23	30.7	34	45.3	8	10.7	-	-
	8th grade (n=75)	49	65.3	22	29.3	35	46.7	8	10.7	2	3.7
	Total (n=225)	139	61.8	67	29.8	106	47.1	36	16.0	5	2.2

X^2=0.751 p>.05 df=2 X^2=0.179 p>.05 df= 2 X^2= 0.268 p>.05 df= 2 X^2=9.092 p<.05 df= 2
LR =4.348 p>.05 df= 2

Reasons behind Children's wanting to Possess the Goods or Services Seen on Advertisements

Among the reasons of children's wanting to possess the goods or services seen on advertisements, "liking the product or services seen on advertisements" lead the first place with a ratio of 61.8 %. On the other hand, "only curiosity" follows the first rank with a ratio of 47.1 % and "liking the advertisements of products and services" take the third place with a ratio of 29.8 % (Table 7).

As it can be seen in Table 7, this issue shows similarities in terms of both gender and grade. "Liking the product or services seen on advertisements" and "only curiosity" take the lead as the reasons for the desire to possess products or services seen on advertisements.

The Situation of Children's Unnecessary Consumption Due to Advertisements

Being frequently confronted with television advertisements, children regard advertisements as the primary source of information. By informing children about the external world, advertisements contribute to the socialization of children. Yet, at the same time they might have negative effects like encouraging children for unnecessary consumption (Doğan, 2003). As a matter of fact, one of the criticisms directed against advertisements is that television advertisements lead children for needless consumption (Savran, 2000).

In the scope of this study, children were asked whether "advertisements cause purchasing products or services that are not needed." While 59.6% answered "sometimes" and 23.6% answered "always" (Table 8).

Table 8. The Situation of Children's Unnecessary Consumption due to Advertisements

Explanatory Variables		The Situation of Children's Unnecessary Consumption due to Advertisements							
		Always		Sometimes		Never		Total	
		n	%	n	%	N	%	n	%
Gender	Female	31	28.7	63	58.3	14	13.0	108	100.0
	Male	22	18.8	71	60.7	24	20.5	117	100.0
	Total	53	23.6	134	59.6	38	16.9	225	100.0
$X^2 = 4.284$ p<.05 df= 2									
Grade	6th grade	18	24.0	48	64.0	9	12.0	75	100.0
	7th grade	16	21.3	43	57.3	16	21.3	75	100.0
	8th grade	19	25.3	43	57.3	13	17.3	75	100.0
	Total	53	23.6	134	59.6	38	16.9	225	100.0
$X^2 = 2.840$ p<.05 df= 4									

In accordance with this finding, Devrez's (1979) study found that advertisements creates a desire for buying and this desire manifests itself in the purchasing of products seen on television advertisements. Similarly, Tokgöz (1982) conducted a study in order to find the effects of advertisements on children in Turkey. The results showed that children are led to extreme consumption through the effects of television advertisements. Likewise, Karaca et.al's (2007) study also determined that 87.6 % of the families complained about advertisements' "directing children towards purchasing goods that are not needed."

As it can be seen Table 8 as well, in both gender groups and all grade levels those who think that advertisements "sometimes" lead to unnecessary consumption are in the first place (P<.05).

The Situation of whether Products and Services Carry the Characteristics Stated in Advertisements

68.8 % of the children answered the question "Do the products and services that you purchased by being affected by advertisements carry the characteristics stated in advertisements?" as "sometimes." On the other hand, only 6.0 % of the children expressed that the good and services they purchase "always" carry the characteristics stated in advertisements (Table 9).

When this subject is investigated in relation to gender; it is found that whereas 72.1 % of girls state that the goods and services that they buy "sometimes" have the characteristics stated in advertisements, this ratio is 65.8 % for boys. The ratio of those who affirm that purchased goods and services "always" carry the characteristics stated in advertisements is the same for girls (2.0 %) and boys (10.0 %) (Table 9). Therefore, findings indicate that girls are less satisfied with the purchased products and services seen on advertisements than boys are. In due course, a statistically significant relationship between this issue and gender was found (P<.05). When the subject matter is analyzed in terms of the grades in which children continue their education, it is seen that the ratio of those who state that goods or services "sometimes" have the characteristics stated in advertisements increases with the increase in grade level (6th grade: 66.7 %, 7th grade: 68.0 %, 8th grade: 72.0 %). The ratio of those who suggest that goods or services "never" have the characteristics stated in advertisements decline with the increase in grade level (6th grade: 30.7 %; 7th grade: 24.0 %, 8th grade: 20.0 %).

Table 9. Children's Views on Whether Products and Services Carry the Characteristics Stated in Advertisements

Explanatory Variables		The Case of Whether Products and Services Carry the characteristics Stated in Advertisements							
		Always		Sometimes		Never		Total	
		n	%	n	%	N	%	n	%
Gender	Female	2	2.0	78	72.1	28	25.9	108	100.0
	Male	12	10.0	77	65.8	28	23.9	117	100.0
	Total	14	6.0	155	68.8	56	24.9	225	100.0
$X^2 = 6.800$ p<.05 df= 2									
Grade	6th grade	2	2.7	50	66.7	23	30.7	75	100.0
	7th grade	6	8.0	51	68.0	1 8	24.0	75	100.0
	8th grade	6	8.0	54	72.0	15	20.0	75	100.0
	Total	14	6.2	155	68.9	56	24.9	225	100.0
LR = 2.798 p>.05 df= 4									

On the other hand, the ratio of those who answer the question "always" increase with the increase in grade level (6th grade: 2.7 %, 7th grade: 8.0 %, 8th grade: 8.0 %) (Table 9). According to these findings, it can be concluded that as the grade level increases, children start to act more rationally in their choice of goods and services; therefore, the goods and services they purchase meet their expectancies more.

Children's Views on Advertisements

The most debated issues in advertising studies are focused upon encouraging people for unnecessary consumption, misguiding people by giving wrong information about the characteristics of the product or the service, exaggerating the benefits of the product or the service, exploiting the emotions of consumers in trying to make them purchase (Elden and Ulukök, 2006).

In this research, while the majority of the children (81.8 %) found advertisements "entertaining," 60.7 % stated that advertisement "causes prodigality" (Table 10).

Analyzing the issue in relation to gender, it is shown that majority of the girls (86.1 %) stated that advertisements are "entertaining," while 80.6 % thought that advertisements are "effective in shopping." Furthermore, 62.6 % of the girls expressed that television advertising "causes prodigality." On the other hand, while 77.8 % of boys said that advertisements are "effective in shopping," 77.8 % find advertisements "entertaining." These are followed by those boys who think that advertisements are "informing and useful" (P<.05) (Table 10).

When the issue is analyzed in relation to the grade level, it is discovered that the ratio of those who find advertisements as "misguiding and deceptive" (6th grade: 40.5 %, 7th grade: 53.3%, 8th grade: 61.3 %), "leading to prodigality" (6th grade: 50.7 %, 7th grade: 62.7 %, 8th grade: 68.9 %) raise with the increase in grade level. At the same time, it is also observed that the ratio of those who think that advertisements are "informing and useful" (6th grade: 65.3 %, 7th grade: 60.0 %, 8th grade: 50.7 %), "honest and believable" (6th grade: 58.7 %, 49.3 %, 8th grade: 45.3%) decrease with the increase in grade level. Moreover, at all grade levels, the ratios of those who find advertisements "entertaining" are close to each other (6th grade: 82.7 %, 7th grade: 80.7 %, 8th grade: 82.7 %) (P<.05) (Table 10). In line with these findings, in a study conducted by Robertson and Rossiter's (1974) it was found that the ratio of those who believe in all advertisements decline with the increase in grade level.

Table 10. Children's Views on Advertisements

Explanatory Variables			It is entertaining		It is informing and useful		It is misguiding and deceptive		It is honest and it believable		It causes prodigality		It is effective in shopping	
			n	%	n	%	N	%	n	%	n	%	n	%
Gender	Female (n=108)	I agree	93	86.1	54	50.0	63	58.9	47	43.5	67	62.6	87	80.6
		I disagree	15	13.9	54	50.0	44	41.1	61	56.5	40	37.4	21	19.4
	Male (n=117)	I agree	91	77.8	78	66.7	53	45.3	68	58.1	69	59.0	92	78.6
		I disagree	26	22.2	39	33.3	64	54.7	49	41.9	48	41.0	25	21.4
	Total (n=225)	I agree	184	81.8	132	58.7	116	51.8	115	51.1	136	60.7	179	79.6
		I disagree	41	18.2	93	41.3	108	48.2	110	48.9	88	39.3	46	20.4
			$X^2 = 10.580$ p<.05 df= 3											
Grade	6th grade (n=75)	I agree	62	82.7	49	65.3	30	40.5	44	58.7	38	50.7	60	80.0
		I disagree	13	17.3	26	34.7	44	59.5	31	41.3	38	49.3	15	20.0
	7th grade (n=75)	I agree	60	80.0	45	60.0	40	53.3	37	49.3	47	62.7	58	77.3
		I disagree	15	20.0	30	40.0	35	46.7	38	50.7	27	37.3	17	22.7
	8th grade (n=75)	I agree	62	82.7	38	50.7	46	61.3	34	45.3	51	68.9	61	81.3
		I disagree	13	17.3	37	49.3	29	38.7	41	54.7	23	31.1	14	18.7
	Total (n=225)	I agree	184	84.8	132	58.7	116	51.8	115	51.1	136	60.7	179	79.6
		I disagree	41	18.2	93	41.3	108	48.2	110	48.9	88	39.3	46	20.4
			$X^2 = 10.580$ p<.05 df= 3											

The findings of this study suggests that as children grow up, they become more aware of the bias and deception in advertisements as well as the persuasive character of advertisements. In fact, many studies shed light upon the fact that as children grow up, their ability to recognize the deceptive, biased and persuasive character of advertisements also develop (John, 1999). Therefore, many studies found a positive relationship between age and understanding the goals of advertisements. To put in other words, as children grow older, their positive feelings towards advertisements turn into negative ones. They even start to doubt and be skeptical of advertisements (Boush, Friestad and Rose, 1994; Ward, Reale and Levinson,1972; Barling and Fullagar, 1983; Elden and Ulukök, 2006; Martin, 1997). For example, in some studies it was shown that starting from the age of 12, children can see advertisements from a critical perspective and understand the intension of producers (Martin, 1997; Peterson and Lewis, 1988; Peterson et al.,1984). More than that, it was also found that they can be skeptical and feel insecurity towards advertisements (Boush, 2001; Van Evra, 1998).

Children's Views Concerning the Necessity of Advertisements

It is observed that 58.2 % of the children within the scope of this study gave the answer "it does not matter" concerning the necessity of advertisements (Table 11). This result indicates that children do not regard advertisements that necessary.

Table 11. Children's Views Concerning the Necessity of Advertisements

Explanatory Variables		Views Concerning the Necessity of Advertisements									
		Very Necessary		It does not matter		Not necessary		No idea		Total	
		N	%	n	%	n	%	n	%	n	%
Gender	Female	20	18.5	70	64.8	16	14.8	2	1.9	108	100.0
	Male	31	26.5	61	52.1	24	20.5	1	0.9	117	100.0
	Total	51	22.7	131	58.2	40	17.8	3	1.3	225	100.0
X^2 4.601 p>.05 df= 3											
Grade	6th grade	24	32.0	36	48.0	13	17.3	2	2.7	75	100.0
	7th grade	16	21.3	46	61.3	13	17.3	-	-	75	100.0
	8th grade	11	14.7	49	65.3	14	18.7	1	1.3	75	100.0
	Total	51	22.7	131	58.2	40	17.8	3	1.3	225	100.0
$X^2 = 9.390$ p>.05 df= 6											

In both gender groups, the ratio of those who stated "it does not matter" is the highest, although the ratio is higher for girls (64.8 %) than for boys (52.1%). In addition to that, the ratios of those, who think that advertisements are "very necessary," are higher in boys (26.5 %) than in girls (18.5 %) (Table 11). When the issue is analyzed in relation to grade levels, it is observed that the ratio of those who find television advertisements "very necessary" decreases with the increase in education level (6th grade: 32.0 %, 7th grade: 21.3 %, 8th grade: 14.7 %). Moreover, the ratio of those who express "it does not matter" concerning the necessity of advertisements' existence raise with the increase in education level (6th grade: 48.0 %, 7th grade: 61.3 %, 8th grade: 65.3 %) (Table 11). This result might stem from the decrease in the ratios of watching television and television advertisements in line with children's growing up.

The Situation Whereby Children Tend to Choose Products or Services That Are More Used or More Liked Although They Are Not Different in Terms of Price or Quality

Most of the children within the scope of this research (89.3 %) stated that when they are confronted with two products or services of no difference in quality or price, they "sometimes" (56.4 %) or "always" (32.9%) tend to choose the one which is more advertised or the one with better advertisements. On the other hand, the ratio of those who "never" (10.7 %) choose the one which is more or better advertised. Generally speaking, this finding indicates that children tend to prefer goods or services seen on television advertisements.

As a matter of fact, Özgen (1989) conducted a research on 300 children in order to understand children's consumption behaviors. In this study, it was found that almost every children (97.0 %) consider television advertisements while doing shopping; thus, television was found to be one of the three information sources that determine children's purchasing behaviors. Similarly, in a study conducted by North and Kotze (2001) results showed that more than one third of the children want to possess the product which is more advertised. In line with these, in researches carried out by Singh (1998) and Jensen (1995) it was underlined that children's choice of products are highly aroused by advertisements.

Table 12. The Situation whereby Children Tend to Choose Products or Services that are More Used or More Liked Although They are not Different in terms of Price or Quality

Explanatory Variables		The Situation whereby Children Tend to Choose Products or Services that are More Used or More Liked Although They are not Different in terms of Price or Quality							
		Always		Sometimes		Never		Total	
		N	%	n	%	n	%	n	%
Gender	Female	33	30.6	66	61.1	9	8.3	108	100.0
	Male	41	35.0	61	52.1	15	12.8	117	100.0
	Total	74	32.9	127	56.4	24	10.7	225	100.0
$X^2 = 2.205$ p>.05 df= 2									
Grade	6th grade	35	46.7	34	45.3	6	8.0	75	100.0
	7th grade	18	24.0	49	65.3	8	10.7	75	100.0
	8th grade	21	28.0	44	58.7	10	13.3	75	100.0
	Total	74	32.9	127	56.4	24	10.7	225	100.0
$X^2 = 10.432$ p<.05 df= 4									

Analyzing the issue in terms of gender difference, it is seen that the ratio of boys who "sometimes" choose the product or service which is more or better advertised take the lead (female: 61.1 %, male: 52.1 %). This is followed by the ratio of those who "always" choose products or services which are more advertised or which have better advertisements (female: 30.6 %, male 35.5 %) (Table 12). When the subject is analyzed in terms of grade levels, it is understood that the ratio of those who "always" choose the product or service that is better and more advertised takes the lead in 6th grade with a ratio of 46.7 %. On the other hand, the first ranks belong to those who "sometimes" choose such products in the 7th (65.3%) and 8th (58.7%) grades. As the level of education increases, the ratio of those who state that they do not choose products and services with better and more advertisements also increases (P<.05) (Table 12). This situation gives the idea that children start to be more impartial in choosing products and services as they grow; therefore, it seems that children start to make their decisions in the light of objective criteria.

CONCLUSION

Children are very crucial for young populated countries like Turkey, because they form a vital market. Therefore, as it can be seen from research findings, they form an important target for advertisers. Various producers and distributers of national or foreign branded products are in a constant attempt to influence this target through advertisements. Yet, when research findings are analyzed in detail with reference to children's abilities to perceive, gather information and be affected, it becomes evident that advertisements might contain various problems concerning children.

On the other hand, being totally against advertisements is inconceivable as well. Advertisements have many useful functions: not only can television play an important role in socialization of children as consumers, but also television advertisements can inform little children about their external worlds. They enable children to enter into the world of objects, specially the world of objects oriented towards adults. In a way, advertisements contribute to the social development of the children as they bring them closer to new objects (Doğan, 2003). With the help of some advertisements, the child remembers once again that he should brush his teeth and that milk is healthy and he should drink it. Therefore, seen from this perspective advertisements are educating and monitory (Karaca, Pekyaman and Güney, 2007).

In due course, society is not reactive against the activities of advertising, rather it opposes to the methods used to enhance the effects of advertisements. Deceptive and misguiding applications are the most important methods among these (Akan, 1995). Since children are vulnerable and in need of protection; controlling, limiting and prohibiting advertisements will be for societal good. However, advertisements still continue to affect children despite the limitations and in fact children are more affected by advertisements than adults are. Thus, public forces have to take action around two alternatives: either marketing stimuli (advertisement) will be controlled or variables that change the effects of these stimuli will be reorganized. The first one refers to auditing, while the second one refers to an education strategy. The effects of advertisements are not the same on every child. They can be either high or low in accordance with parent attention, inter familial relationships and education level. This influence also differs in relation to child's "advertisement consciousness." In that case, some of these variables can be targeted in order to educate the children about advertisements. As these factors ease the effects of advertisement on the child, it is more appropriate to develop these factors in the child and in his environment. These should be organized around two axes. On the one hand, critical capacity of the child should be developed in the face of the messages stemming from the means of advertising and communication. On the other hand, skills to make him a good buyer should be built up. Distancing the child from the message through developing his critical capacity would teach him to understand the images better. Furthermore, it would also enable him to distinguish technique of highlighting techniques through images and voice. In this way, he would learn the persuasive intention of advertisement. As a second goal, education oriented towards equipping the child with skills to make rational choices in buying can decrease the effects of marketing stimuli in the short run. In the long run, this goal is important for the children, as the adults of the future, to develop models for health decision making (Kapferer, 1991). Educating children are necessary, yet not suffici ent. Parents also should try to quit their habits of sitting in front of the television whole day. As parents can quit such habit, they can also save their children and secure them against advertisements to some extend. Being exemplary through action is the most efficient method of education. Besides educating children and self control of parents, advertising agencies should take responsibilities. They should consider the side effects of advertisements and take action accordingly. Children start to make more demands with the effects of advertisements. Yet, families with low income levels find it extremely hard to meet these demands. In addition to that, families with adequate income levels might refuse these demands on the grounds that buying whatever the child wants is not right. This situation might form a feeling of deprivation and offense for the child. Advertisements, which are also called as the online form of consumption capitalism, bring such difficulties with itself (Karaçoşkun, 2009). For this reason, advertisers or advertising agencies should act with social responsibility rather than with a mere focus on the product sales. More specifically, considering that children of young ages are more vulnerable and more affected, advertisements should not include messages that are deceptive, misguiding and encouraging consumption. In due course, having both positive and negative effects advertisements should be processed and controlled in line with basic principles that will be considered in advertisements oriented towards children. Along with this, educating children and people around them about advertisements is of significance.

REFERENCES

AC Nielsen ZET, (1999) Televizyon reklamlarının çocukların ve gençlerin satın alma ve marka kararlarında ki etkisi. http:// *www.bianet.com*

Ahuja, R. D. B., and Stinson, K. M., (1993). Female-headed single parent families: An exploratory study of children's ınfluence in family decision making. *Advances in Consumer Research, 20,* 469-474.

Akan, P., (1995). Reklamcının toplumsal sorumluluğu. *Pazarlama Dünyası, 9, 51,* 17.

Akbulut, N. T., (2004). Reklamın evdeki temsilcisi çocuklar, *http://www. bianet.org/bianet/cocuk/63156-reklamin-cekici-eglendirici-ogesi-cocuklar*

Akçalı, S. (2004). Tüketim toplumunda çocuğun yitişi. *Çoluk Çocuk Dergisi, 34,* 23-24.

Aker, A.O., (1978). In consumerism search for the consumer interest. In. A. Aker Editor, and G.S. Day Editor (Eds). *The social and economic effects of asdvertising.* New York: A Division of Mac Million Pub. Co.

Aksoy, A., and Batmaz,V., (1995). *Türkiye'de televizyon ve aile.* T.C. Başbakanlık Aile Araşırma Kurumu Yayını, İstanbul: Pan Ajans ve İletişim A.Ş.

Arslan, A., (2004). Bir sosyolojik olgu olarak televizyon. *Uluslar arası İnsan Bilimleri Dergisi., 1(1). http://www.insanbilimleri.com/ojs/index.php/uib/ article/view/163/163.*

Atay, M., and Öncü, E., (2003). Elektronik bakıcı: Televizyon. *Çoluk Çocuk Dergisi, 27,*14-17.

Barling, J., and Fullagar, C., (1983). Children's attitudes to television advertisements: A factorial perspective. *Journal of Psychology, 113,* 25–30.

Barry, T. E., and Hansen, R.W., (1973). How race affects children's TV commercials. *Journal of Advertising Research, 13,* 63-67.

Bayraktaroğlu, A., (1999). *Televizyon reklamlarının tüketiciler üzerindeki etkilerinin ölçülmesi: Bankacılık sektöründe bir uygulama.* Dokuz Eylül Üniversitesi Sosyal Bilimler Enstitüsü İşletme Anabilim Dalı Yayımlanmamış Doktora Tezi. İzmir.

Bever, T.G., Smith, M.L., Bengen, B., and Johnson, T.G., (1975). Young viewers' troubling responses to TV ads. *Harvard Business Review, 53,* 119–21.

Bir, A., and Maviş, F. (1988). *Dünya'da ve Türkiye'de reklamcılık ve reklamın gücü.* İstanbul: Bilgi Yayınevi.

spots, and public-service announcements. *Communication Research, 12,* 455–484.

Boush, D. M., (2001). *Mediating advertising effects. Television and the American family.* In J. Bryant and J. A. Bryant (Eds.).

Boush, D. M., Friestad, M., and Rose, G. M., (1994). Adolescent skepticism toward TV advertising and knowledge of advertiser tactics. *Journal of Consumer Research, 21, 1,* 165-175.

Bovee C. L., and Arens W. F. (1986) .*Contemporary advertising*. Homewood Illinois: Richard D. Irwin, Inc.

Brettman, J.R. (1979). *An information processing theory of consumer choice*. USA:Addison-Wesley Publishing Co.Inc.

Buckingham, D.(1993). *Chıldren talking television*. London: Falmerpress.

Budak, H.(2001). *Modern-kapitalist toplumlarda birey-tüketim-reklam ilişkisi*. Selçuk Üniversitesi Sosyal Bilimler Enstitüsü Yayımlanmamış Yüksek Lisans Tezi. Konya.

Buijzen, M., and Valkenburg, P. M., (2003a). The effects of television advertising on materialism, parent-child conflict, and unhappiness: A review of research. *Journal of Applied Developmental Psychology, 24,* 437–456.

Buijzen, M., and Valkenburg, P. M., (2003b). The unintended effects of television advertising: A parent-child survey. *Communication Research, 30,* 483–503.

Caron, A., and Ward, S., (1975). Gift decisions by kids and parents. *Journal of Advertising Research, 1975;15,*15-20.

Cereci, S. (1996). Televizyonun sosyolojik boyutu. İstanbul: Şule Yayınları.

Cesur, S., and Paker, O., (2007). Televizyon ve çocuk: Çocukların tv programlarına ilişkin tercihleri. *E-sosder (Elektronik Sosyal Bilimler Dergisi), 19.*

Çetinkaya,Y.(1993). *Reklamcılık ve manipülasyon*. İstanbul: Ağaç Yayıncılık.

Çıngı, H., (1994). *Örnekleme kuramı*. Ankara: Hacettepe Üniversitesi Fen Fakültesi Basımevi.

Çiğdem, A., and Dikeçligil,MB.,M(1991).a *Aile yazıları 3, birey, kişilik ve toplum*. Ankara: T.C Başbakanlık Aile Araştırma Kurumu Başkanlığı.

Dalbudak, Z., and Zorman, Ö. (2000). *Tüketim ve televizyon reklamları*. Ankara Üniversitesi Ev Ekonomisi Yüksekokulu Yayımlanmamış Yüksek Lisans Tezi. Ankara.

Devrez,G. (1979). *Reklamların etkilerinin ölçülmesi*. Ankara Üniversitesi Siyasal Bilgiler Fakültesi Yayınları No: 435. Ankara: Sevinç Matbaası.

Doğan, M., (2003). *Televizyon reklamlarının çocuklar üzerindeki etkisi*. Yayınlanmamış yüksek lisans tezi. Afyon Kocatepe Üniversitesi, Sosyal Bilimler Enstitüsü, Afyon.

Dunne, M., (1999). The role and ınfluence of children in family holiday decision making. *International Journal of Advertising and Marketing to Children, 1, 3,* 181-191.

Elden, M., and Ulukök, Ö., (2006). Çocuklara yönelik reklamlarda denetim ve etik. *Küresel İletişim Dergisi, 2,* 1-22.

Filizer, P. (1999). *Televizyon reklamlarının çocuklar üzerine etkisi*. Ankara Üniversitesi Ev Ekonomisi Yüksekokulu Yayımlanmamış Yüksek Lisans Tezi. Ankara.

Fromm, E. (1982). *Sahip olmak ya da olmamak*. A. Arıten. (Çev.). İstanbul: Arten Yayınevi.

Galst, J., and White, M., (1976). The unhealthy persuader: The reinforcing value of television and children's purchase-influencing attempts at the supermarket. *Child Development, 47*, 1089 -1096.

Goldberg, M. E., (1990). A quasi-experiment assessing the effectiveness of TV advertising directed to children. *Journal of Marketing Research, 27*, 445–54.

Gorn, G.J., Goldberg, M. E., (1977). The impact of television advertising on children from low-income families. *Journal of Consumer Research, 4*, 86-88.

Gönen, E., and Özgen,Ö. (1988) Tüketici ve reklamlar. *Karınca, 54,623*, 8-10.

Güler, D., (1989). Çocuk, televizyon ve çizgi film, kurgu. *Açık Öğretim Fakültesi İletişim Bilimleri Dergisi, 5*.

Gürel, E. (2004). Pazarlamada yeni eğilim: Çocuklara yönelik pazarlama. *Çoluk Çocuk Dergisi, 34*, 32-35.

Güven,Ö. (1996). *Tüketici hukukunda aldatıcı reklamlar/reklamcılıkta özdenetim: İngiltere örneği*. Ankara: Can Ofset Yayıncılık.

Güzel, A. (2001). *Tüketim toplumu tartışmaları*. Cumhuriyet Üniversitesi Sosyal Bilimler Enstitüsü. Yayımlanmamış Yüksek Lisans Tezi, Sivas.

Holdert, F., and Antonides. G., (1997). Family type effects on household members' decision making. *In Advances in Consumer Research, 24*, 48-54.

Halloran, T., Masson, Brown, and Mc Quail (1973). *Televizyon ve etkileri*. İstanbul: Reklam Matbaası.

Jensen, J.M., (1995). Children's purchase requests and parental responses: results from an exploratory study in Denmark. *European Advances in Consumer Research, 2*, 54-60.

John, D. R., (1999). Consumer socialization of children: A retrospective look at twenty-five years of research. *Journal of Consumer Research, 26*, 183–213.

Kaner, S. (1989). Televizyon reklamları ve çocuklar. *Eğitim Bilimleri Dergisi, 22 (2)*, 785-799.

Kapferer, J. N. (1991). *Çocuk ve reklam*. Ş. Önder (Çev). İstanbul: Afa Yayınları.

Karaca, Y., Pekyaman, A., and Güney, H., (2007). Ebeveynlerin televizyon reklam içeriklerinin çocuklar üzerindeki etkilerini etik açıdan algılamalarına yönelik bir araştırma. *Sosyal Bilimler Dergisi, 2,* 233-205.

Karaçoşkun, M.D., (2009). Bireysel ve toplumsal çözülmede televizyon faktörü üzerine düşünceler. http://turnofftv.tuketiciler.org/makaleler/makale1.doc.

Kavas, A. (1985). Reklamın toplumsal etkileri ve reklamcılıkta toplumsal ve ahlaki sorumluluk düşüncesi. *Verimlilik, 14,4,* 54-75.

Kocabaş, F., and Kocabaş, B. (2004). Televizyon reklamlarının çocuğun sağlığı üzerine etkisi. *Çoluk Çocuk Dergisi, 34,* 28-29.

Kocabaş, F., Elden, M., Yurdakul, N. (2000). *Reklam ve halkla ilişkilerde hedef kitle.* Ankara: İletişim Yayınları.

Koç, A., N., Bodur, M., Borak, E., and Doratlı, M., (1988). *Çocukların tüketici olarak toplumsallaşmalarında televizyon reklamlarının rolü.* Boğaziçi Üniversitesi Projesi. SBE/AD 88-02, Eylül.

Kulen,E. (1990). *Televizyondaki şekerli yiyecek maddesi reklamların ilkokul 3 ve 5. sınıf öğrencileri üzerindeki etkisinin incelenmesi.* Hacettepe Üniversitesi. Sağlık Bilimleri Enstitüsü Yayımlanmamış Yüksek Lisans Tezi. Ankara.

Kunkel, D., and Gantz. W., (1992). Children's television advertising in the multi-channel environment. *Journal of Communication, 42 , 3,* 134-152.

Kunkel, D., Wilcox, B.L., Cantor, J., Palmer, E., Linn, S., and Dowrick, P., (2004). Psychological ıssues in the ıncreasing commercialization of childhood. Report of the APA task force on advertising and children.

Kurtz, D.L. , and Boone, L. E. (1987). *Marketting.* Chicago: The Dreyden Press.

Leonhardt, D., and Kathleen, K., (1997). Hey kid. Buy this. *Business Week, June 30,* 62-67.

Lewis, M. K., and Hill, A. J., (1998). Food advertising on British children's television: A content analysis and experimental study with nine-year olds. *International Journal of Obesity, 22,* 206–214.

Lindstrom, M., and Seybold, P.B., (2003). *Brandchild: Inside the minds of today's global kids: Understanding their relationship with brands.* Kogan Page Limited.

Martin, M. C., (1997). Children's understanding of the ıntent of advertising: A meta-analysis. *Journal of Public Policy and Marketing, 16, 2,* 205-216.

Mattelard, A., (1992). *Reklamcılık.* F.Ersoy (Çev.). İstanbul: İletişim Yayınları.

Mengü, S., and Karadogan, E., (2003). *The influence of trust in commercials on brand perception of children.* 1. Uluslararası çocuk ve iletisim konferansı'nda sunulmus bildiri. İstanbul Üniversitesi.

Mete, M., (2004). *Televizyon reklamlarının Türk toplumu üzerindeki etkisi.* Ankara: AKM Başkanlığı Yayınları.

Mitchell, A. A., (1986). The effect of verbal and visual components of advertisements on brand attitudes and attitudes toward the advertisement. *Journal of Consumer Research, 13*, 12-24.

Moore, E. S., and Lutz, R. J., (2000). Children, advertising, and product experiences: A multimethod inquiry. *Journal of Consumer Research, 27, 1,* 31-48.

North, E.J., and Kotze, T., (2001). Parents and television advertisements as consumer socialisation agents for adolescents: An exploratory study. *Journal of Family Ecology and Consumer Sciences, 29*, 91-99.

Özdiker, C., (2004). Çocuk ve televizyon. *Çoluk Çocuk Dergisi, 27*, 18-21.

Özgen, Ö., (1989). Özel tüketici grupları. *Verimlilik Dergisi*, 12, 21-24.

Özgen, Ö., (1995). *Çocuk tüketicilerin sosyalizasyonu.* YA-PA Okul Öncesi Eğitimi ve Yaygınlaştırılması Semineri, 22-25 Mayıs, Ankara, YA-PA Yayın Pazarlama, İstanbul, 353-362.

Öztürk, İ. (1996). *Ebeveyenlerin çocuklarının seyrettikleri televizyon programları ve reklamlarla ilgili düşünceleri.* Ankara Üniversitesi Ev Ekonomisi Yüksekokulu Yayımlanmamış Yüksek Lisans Tezi. Ankara.

Özyurt, İ. (2004). *Ticari reklam ve ilanlarda karşılaştırma ve kötüleme.* Ankara: TC: Sanayi ve Ticaret Bakanlığı Tüketicinin ve Rekabetin Korunması Genel Müdürlüğü.

Peterson, L., and Lewis, K. E., (1988). Preventive intervention to improve children's discrimination of the persuasive tactics in televised advertising. *Journal of Pediatric Psychology, 13, 2,* 163-170.

Peterson, P. E., Jeffrey, D. B., Bridgwater, C. A., and Dawson, B., (1984). How pro-nutrition television programming affects children's dietary habits. *Developmental Psychology, 20, 1*, 55-63.

Pira, A., and Sohodol, Ç., (2004). Reklamlarda çocuğun kullanılması. *Çoluk Çocuk Dergisi, 34*, 27-28.

Revue, (1998). *Sciences at Avenir, February.* (From Kuruoğlu, H., (2009) Televizyonun çocuklar üzerindeki olumsuz etkileri. http://www.sozcu.net/anne-ve-bebek/93266-televizyonun-cocuklar-uzerindeki-olumsuz-etkileri.html)

Robertson, T. S., and Rossiter, J. R., (1973). Children's responsiveness to commercials. *Journal of Communication, 27,* 101-106.

Robertson, T.S., and Rossiter, J. R., (1974). Children and commercial persuasion: An attribution theory analysis. *The Journal of Consumer Research, 1, 1,* 13-20.

Robertson, T.S., and Ward, S., and Gatignon, H. and Klees, D.M. (1989). Advertising and children: A cross-cultural study. *Communication Research, 16(4),* 459-485.

Robinson, T. N., and Saphir, M. N., and Kraemer, H. C., and Varady, A., and Haydel, K.F. (2001). Effects of reducing television viewing on children's requests for toys. A randomized controlled trial, *Journal of Development and Behavioural Pediatrics, 3, 22.*

RTÜK (2004). *Reklamların izleyiciler üzerindeki etkileri.* Ankara: Tisamet Yayınevi.

Rutherford, P. (1998). *Yeni İkonlar/Televizyon reklam sanatı.* İstanbul: Yapıkredi Yayınları.

Saatçiler, C., (1997). *Anaokuluna giden çocukların sosyalizasyon sürecinde ebeveynlerin ve eğiticilerin rolü.* Ege Üniversitesi Sosyal Bilimler Enstitüsü Basılmamış Yüksek Lisans Tezi. İzmir.

Savran, B., (2000). Reklamlar *ve tıbbi etik. Türkiye Klinikleri Journal of Medical Ethics, 8,* 23-27.

Sheikh, A.A., and Moleski, L. M., (1977). Conflict in the family over commercials. *Journal of Communication, 27,* 152-157.

Singh, D., (1998). Children as consumers. *Indian Management, September,* 78-81.

Suna, H. (1963). *Televizyon ve şiddetin çocuk üzerine etkisini fark edin.* İstanbul: İrfan Yayınevi.

Tokgöz, O. (1980). *Televizyon reklamları ve çocuklar.* Ankara: Ankara Üniversitesi Siyasal Bilgiler Fakültesi Basın Yayın Yüksek Okulu Basımevi.

Tokgöz, O.(1982). *Televizyon reklamlarının anne çocuk ilişkisine etkileri.* Ankara Üniversitesi Basın ve Yayın Yüksek Okulu Yayımlanmış Doktora Tezi.Ankara.

Turan, E. (1996). *Ekranaltı çocukları/televizyon ve toplum.* İstanbul:İrfan Yayınevi.

Uebert, M., and Meare, J. M, and Davidson, E. S. (1973). *Early window effect of television on children and youth.* Newyork: Pegamaon Press.

Unnikrishnan, N., and Baipai, S., (1996). *The impact of television advertising on children.* New Delhi: Sage Publication.

Ünsal, Ö. (2000). Reklam, hayatlar ve yansımalar. *Görüş Dergisi, Eylül ,* 17-18.

Valkenburg, P. M., (2000). Media and youth consumerism. *Journal of Adolescent Health, 27, 2,* 52-56.

Van Evra, J., (1998). *Television and child development.* London: Erlbaum.

Ward, S., Reale, G., and Levinson, D. (1972). *Children's perceptions, explanations and judgements of television advertising: A further exploration.* In E. A. Rubinstein, G. A. Comstock, and J. P. Murray, (Eds). Washington DC: Government Printing Office.

Ward, S., Wackman, D., and Wartella, E., (1977). *How children learn to buy: The development of consumer information-processing skills.* Beverly Hills, CA: Sage.

Ward, S., Wackman, D., (1972). Television advertising and intra-family influence: Children's purchase influence attempts and parental yielding. *Journal of Marketing Research, 9,* 316-319.

Williams, L.A., and A. Veeck., (1998). An exploratory study of children's purchase influence in urban China. *Asia Pacific Advances in Consumer Research, 3,* 13-19.

Yavas, U., and Abdul-Gader, A., (1993). Impact of TV commercials on Saudi children's purchase behaviour. *Marketing Intelligence and Planning, 11, 2,* 37-43.

Yengin, H. (1994). *Ekranın büyüsü.* İstanbul . Der Yayınevi.

Young, B., (2003). Does food advertising influence children's food choices? A critical review of some of the recent literature. *International Journal of Advertising, 22,* 441- 459.

Yulafçı, A. (2002). *İletişim bilimleri açısından reklamı anlamak.* Marmara Üniversitesi Sosyal Bilimler Enstitüsü. Yayımlanmamış Yüksek Lisans Tezi. İstanbul.

In: Advertising
Editor: Evelyn P. Mann

ISBN 978-1-61324-679-5
© 2012 Nova Science Publishers, Inc.

Expert Commentary

ALCOHOL ADVERTISING ON THE INTERNET: RISKS FOR UNDERAGE YOUTH

Jennifer A. Epstein[1] and Nancy P. Barnett[2]
[1]Weill Cornell Medical College, NYC, NY, U.S.A.
[2]Brown University, Providence, RI, U.S.A.

ABSTRACT

The internet is an important medium for advertising; web advertisements provide income for web sites, online e-mail services and search engines, and are considerably less expensive than other forms of advertising. Advertisements are intended to influence the behavior of the internet user, but in some cases may expose the viewer to images or issues that are not age appropriate.

Advertisements are common on social network sites, yet information from companies may not always be openly identified as an advertisement. For example, when a user indicates "liking" some online content or becoming a member of a particular group, they may be later targeted for specific messages from advertisers or employees of the company selling the product.

Young users of social network web pages, such as Facebook, may not realize that if they indicate they "like" an alcohol product (or become a member of a related group) they are more likely to receive messages from alcohol companies. In this commentary, we discuss the reach of internet advertising, the marketing of alcohol products on the internet, and its possible influence on youth.

Computers and the use of the internet have become commonplace, and adoption in homes in the United States has been faster than earlier technologies such as the telephone or television. According to Watkins (2009), "the diffusion of the Internet in American homes was considerably more rapid then the computer…by making the Internet a much more visual, dynamic, and creative experience, broadband also made it more directly competitive to television." Watkins (2009) also observes that by the late 1990s, desire to access the internet was the primary reason for purchasing a computer. By 2010, the national Pew Internet and American Life Project found that 93% of teens and young adults were using the internet (Purcell, 2010). The internet has increasingly become a location for acquiring information, a method for communicating (using e-mail/instant messaging), and a way to socialize (via chat rooms, social networking sites, etc.).

As internet use has become more common, advertising methods using the internet have grown. Common advertising approaches include the use of (1) sidebar ads; (2) popup ads, (3) ads in e-mail, and (4) websites designed by marketers to advertise a product. Unlike advertising in other more established forms of media, including print (magazines, newspapers), radio, and television, advertising on the internet is more interactive, targeted to individuals, and less expensive. For example, advertisers can present different images and text according to website user demographics. Products that are outside of the mainstream, have a special appeal to a particular target audience, or are illicit or illegal may be more likely to be advertised on the internet. The anonymity of internet communication, the ease of putting up and taking down websites, the ability to have multiple sites with the same purpose are attractive to individuals or groups who take a mass marketing approach. It is our belief that the advertisement on the internet is also more likely than other methods to be inappropriately targeting subgroups. This may be true of a variety of products, but this commentary will focus on the presentation of alcohol advertisements to adolescents and young adults under the legal drinking age.

Due to their high use of the internet in general and social networking sites in particular, youth may be at special risk of being exposed to alcohol-related advertising, despite being under the legal drinking age of 21 (in the United States). On the one hand, assuming there are no controls installed on a computer (e.g., parental controls that limit access to sites or software), an adolescent can voluntarily access sites that advertise alcohol. However, on some sites, such as social networking sites, users must enter their birthdate to join, so in cases like these, the website itself can control the content its users see. In one example of how alcohol is promoted on the social networking site Facebook, researchers created two fictitious user profiles – one that was over 21 and the other that was under 21. Both profiles listed alcohol-related terms under interests and activities. Both users were able to join alcohol-related pages, use alcohol-related applications, including those that were sponsored by alcohol brands or bars, and join groups that advertised alcohol and/or events sponsored by alcohol companies (Mart, Mergendoller and Simon, 2009). This study's findings demonstrate how easily underage internet users can be exposed to alcohol-related advertising. Facebook has faced considerable criticism regarding its policy on providing user private information to advertisers.

Facebook's response by Elliot Schrage, vice president for public policy was featured in the New York Times on May 11th, 2010:

> Advertising. Sponsorship. I think people still ask because the ads complement, rather than interrupt, the user experience. They think, "That can't be it." It is. The privacy implications of our ads, unfortunately, appear to be widely misunderstood. People assume we're sharing or even selling data to advertisers. We're not. We have no intention of doing so. If an advertiser targets someone interested in boats, we'll serve ad impressions to people with 'boats' on their profile somewhere. However, we don't provide the advertiser any names or other personal information about the Facebook users who view or even click on the ads. Anonymized demographically targeted ads work. We like them. You should, too. As a result, advertisers are willing to pay to reach this audience without needing personal data.

Although it addresses the sale of personal information to advertisers, this answer does not address the issue of alcohol being advertised or promoted through alcohol groups to underage youth. In addition, users may not understand that the information they include in their profiles is being used to target advertising. The age policies restrict those under the age of 13 (for Facebook and other social networking sites) but there is apparently no check on age for targeting alcohol advertisements, promotions or allowing a user to join an alcohol-related group. This is in contrast to the way alcohol companies conduct promotions in person: they must have parental permission to allow under-age youth to receive products like baseball caps, magnets, and the like that promote the alcohol product.

In addition to the exposure to alcohol content on social networking sites, some web-based e-mail relies on targeted advertising depending upon what the user is writing in e-mail messages. For example, using online e-mail providers, users who use words such as "beer," "wine" or "alcohol" may start receiving alcohol-related advertising in their e-mail messages (seen only by the sender but not by the recipient of the e-mail). Again these ads may be reaching people under the legal drinking age.

Studies have linked the use of traditional advertising and promotions to underage alcohol use, and it is highly likely that similar effects would be found with alcohol-related internet-based advertising. Methods need to be developed to prevent the presentation of age inappropriate advertising on the internet and to educate youth about the effects of these messages. It has been suggested that users need to prove that they are of legal drinking age, as they do in person, though this would appear to be difficult to achieve in the online world. One suggestion has been to ask youth for their birthdate on two separate occasions, this too is by no means a cure, in that underage youth may lie about their age. Some sites require use of a credit card to prove an adult is involved, but this would not properly address proof of drinking age of 21 in the United States. Given the practices of online advertisement approaches, and the lack of protections in place for underage youth, training in media resistance skills may prove beneficial in teaching underage youth techniques to help them combat the media onslaught (Epstein and Botvin, 2008).

REFERENCES

Epstein, J.A. and Botvin, G.J. (2008). Media resistance skills and drug skill refusal techniques: What is their relationship with alcohol use among inner-city adolescents? *Addictive Behaviors, 33,* 528-537.

Mart, M., Mergendoller, J. and Simon,M. (2009). Alcohol promotion on Facebook. *The Journal of Global Drug Policy and Practice, 3(3)* http://globaldrugpolicy. org/3/3/1.php.

New York Times (2010). http://bits.blogs.nytimes.com/2010/05/11/facebook-executive-answers-reader-questions/

Purcell, K. (2010). Teens and the internet: The future of digital diversity. Pew Internet and American Life Project. http://www.pewinternet.org/ Presentations /2010/Mar/Fred-Forward.aspx

Watkins, S.C. (2009). *The Young and the Digital: What the Migration to Social Network Sites, Games, and Anytime, Anywhere Media Means for Our Future.* Beacon Press: Boston, MA.

INDEX

DATE DUE	RETURNED